SALES CONFIDENCE THAT LASTS

How Professionals Stay Calm, Credible, and in Control Under Pressure

By J.M. Walsh

Author: J. M. Walsh
Publisher: Breakthrough Publishing
Copyright Owner: Breakthrough Change Management

ISBN (Paperback): 978-1-9193918-9-2
ISBN (eBook): 978-1-918502-00-8

Contents

CHAPTER 1: Why Sales Feels Uncomfortable and Why That's Normal

Understanding the emotional reality of selling *1*

CHAPTER 2: The Emotional Realities of Selling

Why Even Good Salespeople Feel the Strain *8*

CHAPTER 3: Steadying Yourself Before You Meet the Customer

How to Enter Every Interaction with Calm, Quiet Confidence *15*

CHAPTER 4: Understanding Your Self-Talk

Where It Comes From and How to Take Back Control *21*

CHAPTER 5: Planning, Preparation, and Mental Rehearsal

How Professionals Build Confidence Before the Customer Arrives *27*

CHAPTER 6: Handling Pressure in the Moment

How to Stay Composed, Clear, and in Control When It Matters Most *34*

CHAPTER 7: Handling Rejection Without Losing Confidence

How to Stay Motivated, Professional, and Grounded When Customers Say "No" *40*

CHAPTER 8: Managing Quiet Days Without Losing Momentum

Why Low Activity Is Risky and How Professionals Stay in Control *47*

CHAPTER 9: Managing End-of-Season Fatigue

How to Stay Effective, Energised, and Confident When Your Tank Is Running Low *53*

CHAPTER 10: Handling Difficult Customers with Confidence

How to Stay Calm, Professional, and in Control When People Test You *59*

CHAPTER 11: Confidence as a Professional Identity

What Changes When Confidence Stops Being Conditional *66*

CHAPTER 12: Recovering from Mistakes Without Losing Confidence

Why Errors Don't Damage Confidence Self-Judgement Does.............................72

CHAPTER 13: The Emotional Patterns That Shape Your Confidence

How Confidence Is Built or Undermined Over Time...78

CHAPTER 14: The Behaviours That Sustain Confidence

What Confident Professionals Do Consistently Even on Ordinary Days 83

CHAPTER 15:Communicating With Confidence

How Confident Salespeople Sound, Speak, and Connect Without Forcing It 89

CHAPTER 16: Trust, Consistency, and Long-Term Relationships

How Confident Salespeople Turn One Conversation Into a Lifetime of Business................95

CHAPTER 17: Thinking Like a Confident Professional

How to Build a Mindset That Supports You for a Lifetime in Sales................................102

CHAPTER 18: The Confidence Cycle

How to Protect, Renew, and Strengthen Your Confidence for Life 109

A Final Invitation 114

About the Author 115

Further Reading.. 116

CHAPTER 1:

Why Sales Feels Uncomfortable and Why That's Normal

Understanding the emotional reality of selling

The young woman standing in the doorway leading out to the caravan showground looked about twenty-three. First week on the job, maybe first day. I was there consulting with the sales team, and I watched her spot a couple getting out of their car in the car park. She straightened her jacket, took a breath, and started walking toward them.

Then she stopped. Just froze for a moment, mid-stride. Her hand went to her hair, adjusting it unnecessarily. She glanced back at the office, as if checking whether anyone was watching. The couple were ten feet away from her, hadn't noticed her yet. She took another breath - deeper this time - and moved toward them, but something had shifted in her posture. The confidence she'd gathered had leaked away in those three seconds of hesitation.

I've seen that moment thousands of times. That flicker of uncertainty that shows up just before you step into a conversation with someone who hasn't decided who you are yet. It doesn't matter whether it's your first day or your tenth year - that moment exists. The internal voice that whispers: *What if they don't like me? What if I can't answer their questions? What if I say the wrong thing?*

The couple walked in. She greeted them professionally, did everything right technically, asked decent questions, explained the products clearly. But the hesitation from those three seconds in the doorway never quite left her. You could hear it in her pace - slightly too fast, as if she was rushing to prove

1

something. You could see it in how she filled every silence, adding explanations that weren't needed. The couple were polite, took a brochure, said they'd think about it, and left.

Afterward, she came back to the office and sat down heavily. "I don't know why I find this so hard," she said to no one in particular. "I know the product. I know what to say. But the moment I see someone walking toward me, something just... happens."

What she was describing wasn't weakness. It was biology colliding with the demands of a role that most people's nervous systems weren't designed for.

Every salesperson remembers the early days. The first cold call. The first customer who walks into the shop or showroom. The first time you approach someone on the floor, step onto a site, or walk into a client's office.

There is a moment often brief, but unmistakable when you find yourself face-to-face with a complete stranger and are expected to act as if you belong there.

Even years later, that moment hasn't disappeared entirely. A new customer enters the space someone who hasn't yet decided whether to like you, trust you, or challenge you and your system prepares itself before your words have fully formed. Sales asks you to step into uncertainty every single day, whether customers come to you or you go to them. That is exactly why confidence matters so much in this profession.

What Nobody Explains at the Start

What's striking is how little of this is acknowledged at the beginning of a sales career. You are trained on the product. You are shown the sales process. You are told what to say. You are shown how the system works. You are taught how to close. But almost nobody teaches you how to deal with yourself.

No one prepares you for:

- The nerves that appear without warning
- The doubts that surface at awkward moments
- The internal self-critique
- The emotional weight of meeting strangers repeatedly
- The pressure of being assessed, often silently

Sales feels uncomfortable because you are human, not because you lack ability.

When you understand why the job triggers the reactions it does, something important shifts. You stop interpreting normal emotional responses as weakness. You stop fighting yourself and confidence begins to grow on a stable foundation rather than a fragile one.

The Psychology of Meeting Strangers

Humans are not naturally designed to meet a constant stream of new people. For most of our evolutionary history, we lived in small, predictable communities typically fewer than 150 individuals. This idea is often referred to as *Dunbar's Number*. Whether the number itself is precise doesn't matter. What matters is the principle: our brains evolved for familiarity, not for endless introductions. Sales breaks that pattern every single day.

You meet strangers continuously. You initiate conversations without knowing how the other person feels. You enter interactions without knowing what they expect or how they will respond. You are dealing with people who may arrive guarded, sceptical, distracted, defensive, rushed, or disinterested often before you have said a single word.

This creates discomfort not because you are unsuited to the role, but because your nervous system is doing exactly what it was designed to do: scanning unfamiliar situations for potential risk.

Confidence begins to grow when you recognise this instead of resisting it. Discomfort does not mean something is wrong. It becomes manageable when you see it as part of the job rather than a flaw in your character.

The Fear of Being Judged

Sales places you in front of an audience every day. When you meet a customer, you know often subconsciously that you are being assessed:

- Your appearance
- Your tone
- Your credibility
- Your professionalism
- Your intent

This feels risky for a deep psychological reason. Historically, social rejection threatened survival. Humans lived in groups, and exclusion carried real danger. Although the world has changed, the psychological mechanisms have not.

Your body reacts to the possibility of judgement as if something far more serious than a sale is at stake. That's why the same questions surface repeatedly:

- Will they like me?
- Will they trust me?
- Will this go well?
- Will I handle this properly?

This is not insecurity. It is biology.

Confidence does not come from pretending that internal alarm isn't there. It comes from learning not to overreact to it. You learn to notice the signal without letting it dictate your behaviour. You separate the emotional response from the professional task. Over time, what once felt threatening becomes something you can navigate with steadiness and maturity.

Why Sales Can Feel Like Being "On Stage"

Sales does not just expose you to new people. It places you into a role where you are expected to lead. You are expected to:

- Guide the conversation
- Understand needs that may not yet be clear
- Remain composed, even when the customer is not
- Answer questions clearly
- Handle objections with professionalism
- Support decisions that may carry emotional or financial weight

In many ways, you are performing not theatrically, but professionally. You are presenting ideas, interpreting signals, managing energy, calming uncertainty, and building trust in real time. You are doing this without a script, in front of people whose expectations you cannot fully see. That level of exposure naturally creates pressure.

Even highly competent salespeople experience moments where confidence dips. Not because they lack skill, but because they are repeatedly required to operate in full view of another person's judgement. Confidence is not the absence of this pressure. It is the ability to perform well despite it.

Why People Get Nervous Meeting Customers

Every new customer brings uncertainty. You don't know:

- What they want
- What they are worried about
- What they expect from you
- Whether they are open or defensive
- What kind of day they've had

Uncertainty is one of the strongest triggers of the stress response. Humans are wired to prefer predictability. Sales denies you that comfort. You must stay calm without knowing the outcome. You must lead without full information. You must remain steady while the situation unfolds in real time.

Confidence grows when you become comfortable operating inside uncertainty not by eliminating it, but by staying grounded in the middle of it. This ability is one of the most powerful professional skills a salesperson can develop.

Why Understanding This Comes Before Confidence

Many people believe confidence is simply a matter of personality or willpower as if some people naturally have it and others must struggle without it. But confidence cannot grow on top of shame, confusion, or unrealistic expectations.

If you believe you should feel comfortable in situations where discomfort is normal, you create unnecessary pressure on yourself. You begin to misinterpret normal human reactions as personal failure. Confidence begins with understanding.

When you understand:

- Why nerves appear
- Why meeting strangers feels stressful
- Why judgement stings
- Why certain customers shake you
- Why doubt can appear even when you are skilled

That's when, you stop fighting your own psychology. The discomfort does not disappear, but it stops defining you. It becomes part of the job, not part of your identity. That is the shift from fragile confidence to durable confidence. The kind that holds under pressure. The kind you can rely on.

A Foundation for What Follows

This chapter lays the foundation for everything else in this book. You now understand why sales feels uncomfortable, why confidence fluctuates, and why normal human responses often masquerade as self-doubt. With this grounding, the emotional realities of selling become easier to navigate.

In **Chapter 2**, we move deeper into those realities: the awkwardness, the hesitation, the pressure of performance, and the psychological patterns that shape confidence day to day. The better you understand your internal landscape, the more effectively you can influence your confidence calmly, deliberately, and without pretending to be someone you're not. This understanding doesn't remove the pressure of sales it explains it.

CHAPTER 2:

The Emotional Realities of Selling

Why Even Good Salespeople Feel the Strain

Sales is a demanding profession in ways most people never see. If you have ever felt drained, anxious, hesitant, frustrated, or quietly depleted by this work, there is nothing wrong with you. You are experiencing the normal emotional load of a role that asks far more of people psychologically than most jobs ever will.

This chapter lays out that reality clearly and without drama. Not to make excuses, and not to make the job sound harder than it is but to help you understand what you are actually managing every day. Once you see it properly, something important happens you stop taking the strain personally and start handling it professionally.

You Meet People Who Haven't Decided Who You Are Yet

Every customer arrives with their own history. Their past experiences with salespeople. Their expectations. Their assumptions. Their frustrations. Some arrive friendly. Some arrive cautious. Some arrive guarded. Some arrive ready for conflict not because of you, but because of what came before you. You walk into that uncertainty every time.

In most professions, credibility arrives before you do. A nurse walks into a patient's room with the authority of their uniform and institution. A teacher enters a classroom where their role is already understood and respected. A solicitor sits down with clients whose trust is provisionally granted by credentials and regulation.

Salespeople face the opposite problem.

Not only do you lack institutional credibility, but you also often walk into active suspicion. The word 'salesperson' itself can trigger defensiveness. Many customers arrive already guarded, shaped by previous experiences of being pressured, misled, or manipulated by someone in your role. Some expect an agenda. Others are cynical before you speak. Many are defensive before you've done anything to warrant it.

You meet people who haven't decided who you are yet, but who may have already decided what salespeople generally are.

And your job is to remain calm, professional, and composed while earning trust that others receive automatically, while overcoming suspicion that others never face, and while being assessed not just on your words but against every poor sales interaction that came before you.

That is emotional labour. It requires strength, not personality

You Are Assessed Quickly and Constantly

Customers make rapid judgements, often unconsciously:

- Are you genuine?
- Do I trust you?
- What's your agenda?
- Are you pushing me?
- Are you competent?

This assessment happens whether you like it or not. Most people dislike being judged. Sales asks you to walk into judgement willingly and repeatedly. The emotional challenge is not avoiding that reality but staying steady inside it. Confidence is not the absence of nerves. Confidence is the ability to remain composed while being evaluated.

People Will Test You, Challenge You, or Distrust You

Sales creates tension because customers want several things at once:

- They want clarity
- They want honesty
- They want control
- They want safety
- They want value

And they do not want to be misled. So, they test you. Sometimes subtly, sometimes directly, sometimes aggressively. You will meet people who assume you are hiding something, working an angle, or preparing to pressure them. Your job is to remain composed while demonstrating otherwise.

This is not personal. It's the role. It's the customer's fear of making a bad decision. It's their history, not your character. When you understand this, you stop reacting defensively and start responding professionally.

Not Everyone Is Honest and You Still Have to Stay Grounded

One of the harder truths in sales is that not every customer tells the full truth. Some withhold information, some avoid commitment, some say one thing and mean another, some play for time and some keep options open without saying so.

Usually not because they are bad people, but because they are protecting themselves. They fear being sold to. They want to avoid discomfort. They want to stay in control. This feels personal. The customer's guardedness, their suspicion, their defensive tone, it lands as if it's about you.

But here's what's actually happening: you're not experiencing their behaviour directly. You're experiencing your thinking about their behaviour. The discomfort you feel isn't coming from them. It's being created, moment to moment, by the meaning your mind assigns to what's happening.

This is the insight that changes everything: thought creates your experience, not circumstances.

When you see this, really see it, you don't have to work at staying detached. Distance appears naturally. The customer's defensiveness doesn't change. But it stops feeling threatening because you've recognised where the threat was being manufactured. Not out there. In here.

That recognition alone shifts your state. Not through effort. Through understanding.

But you do have to navigate it with calmness, maturity, and steadiness. That is where confidence lives not in certainty, but in your ability to stay grounded when the interaction is not clean.

Rejection Is Part of the Job and It Lands Because You Care

Salespeople experience rejection more often than most people realise. Sometimes politely, sometimes abruptly, sometimes disrespectfully. No matter how experienced you are, rejection lands somewhere inside you. Not because you are fragile, but because you care about doing your job well and being seen accurately. Psychologically, rejection activates the same neural pathways as physical pain. The response is real.

The critical distinction is this: rejection is not a verdict on you. It is information about the moment.

- The timing
- The fit
- The need
- The budget
- The mood
- The circumstances

Confidence grows when you stop treating rejection as identity and start treating it as data.

You Are Expected to Ask Questions Most People Avoid

Selling requires asking direct questions that everyday social life teaches people to avoid:

- "What budget are you working with?"
- "What's stopping you from deciding?"
- "Is this a yes or a no today?"
- "What concerns do you still have?"

These questions can feel intrusive, even when asked professionally. That discomfort is not a flaw in you. It is the emotional reality of guiding decisions. Confidence grows when you learn to ask strong questions calmly without fear, apology, or aggression.

Awkward and Confrontational Moments Are Guaranteed

In sales, uncomfortable moments are not exceptions. They are built into the job:

- A customer pushes back unfairly
- Someone goes silent
- Someone becomes defensive
- Someone challenges your credibility
- Someone tries to dominate the interaction

Most people encounter moments like this occasionally. Salespeople encounter them weekly more often daily. Confidence in these situations is not about overpowering the customer. It is about staying centred enough to manage the moment without losing yourself. That is a learnable skill, and we will return to it later in the book.

You Still Have to Sell on Days You Don't Feel Like It

Every salesperson has days when:

- You are tired
- You are flat
- You are distracted by personal issues
- A previous interaction has knocked your confidence

And yet the job expects you to reset quickly and show up again with presence and composure. This is emotional athleticism. You are performing under the weight of your own life while carrying the expectations of others. Confidence grows when you learn how to reset in moments, not days.

You're Expected to Stay Positive in Environments That Aren't

Customers can be rude, dismissive, rushed, suspicious, distracted, or unfair. And in the middle of that, you are expected to remain:

- Professional
- Patient
- Clear
- Composed
- Respectful
- Confident

That is not forced positivity. It is emotional strength. When you recognise this, you stop beating yourself up for feeling tired at the end of the day.

Bringing It All Together

Sales is not hard because you are weak. Sales is hard because it exposes you to constant psychological friction. You absorb other people's stress. You navigate uncertainty and on occasion mild dishonesty from customers or their inability to tell you what they are honestly thinking or feeling.

You are assessed constantly. You invest care where outcomes are uncertain. You experience rejection that triggers real emotional responses and yet, you are expected to stay steady throughout.

When you understand this, something shifts. You stop asking *"What's wrong with me?"* and start recognising the strength the role demands. Confidence begins to grow not by denying the strain, but by understanding it. You are not soft for finding this demanding. You are realistic for recognising what the job requires.

Where We Go Next

Now that you understand the emotional landscape of selling, **Chapter 3** takes you into the practical work of preparing yourself mentally for customer interactions.

You'll learn how to steady your nervous system before stepping into uncertainty, how to remain grounded during difficult moments, and how to develop the kind of calm, quiet confidence that customers trust because it is real not performed.

Steadying Yourself Before You Meet the Customer

How to Enter Every Interaction with Calm, Quiet Confidence

From this point on, the book becomes practical. This chapter and the following ones focus on how confident professionals prepare, regulate themselves, and stay steady in real situations.

Confidence is not built in the moment you meet the customer. It is built in the moments before. The breath you take, the pace you choose, the intention you hold, the state you enter the interaction in. Most salespeople walk into customer conversations reacting to whatever their mind throws at them. Confident salespeople walk in prepared mentally anchored, steady, and present.

This chapter is about that anchoring. Not rituals, routines, or psyching yourself up, but the quiet internal preparation that allows you to lead the interaction rather than react to it. You don't need to become bigger, you don't need to generate energy, you don't need to force confidence. What you need in these moments is steadiness.

Why Nerves Rise Before You Say a Word

Before the customer even appears, your mind starts working ahead:

- *What if they're difficult?*
- *What if they're not interested?*
- *What if I mess this up?*
- *What if they challenge me?*

This isn't a flaw. It's anticipation. Your brain is not warning you about the customer; it's reacting to uncertainty. Evolution trained us to overprepare for risk because risk once meant danger. Today the "risk" is social, emotional, or reputational but the same systems still activate. So, before you speak, your body may produce:

- Faster breathing
- Tightness in the stomach or chest
- A quicker heartbeat
- Racing thoughts
- An urge to avoid or rush the interaction

None of this means you lack confidence. It means your nervous system is doing its job. Confidence is learning how to bring yourself back into a steady state before the conversation begins.

The Customer Feels Your State Before They Hear Your Words

Customers respond to your state before they respond to your message.

They pick up on:

- Your pace
- Your tone
- Your energy
- Your composure
- Your presence

These signals are transmitted instantly. If you enter the interaction rushed, flustered, or mentally scattered, the customer senses it and mirrors it. If you enter calm, grounded, and steady, the customer relaxes with you. This is why preparation matters. It doesn't just affect you it shapes the emotional tone of the entire interaction.

Preparing Yourself Mentally (Without Psyching Yourself Up)

Many people think preparation means boosting themselves getting energised, hyped, or mentally "on." That approach often backfires. It increases pressure, accelerates thinking, and raises expectations. The goal is not to become more intense. The goal is to become steadier. Mental preparation for confidence means:

- Slowing your inner pace
- Reducing mental noise
- Grounding your attention
- Focusing on the next step, not the whole interaction
- Choosing calm over urgency

You don't need to overpower uncertainty. You just need to stop feeding it.

The Power of a Single, Clear Intention

Before any customer interaction, set one intention. Not a list. Not a checklist. Just one.

Examples:

- *Listen first*
- *Stay steady*
- *I'm here to understand*
- *One step at a time.*

A single intention cuts through mental clutter. It gives your mind a direction rather than a demand. When the interaction becomes challenging, you return to that intention instead of getting pulled into reaction. This is not positive thinking. It is focus.

One Slow Breath Changes the State

Your body and mind are tightly connected. When your breath speeds up, your mind speeds up. When your breath slows down, your mind follows. Before meeting a customer, take **one** slow breath in through the nose and out through the mouth.

That single breath is enough to:

- Lower tension
- Steady your nervous system
- Soften your internal pace
- Bring you into the present moment

You don't need a breathing technique. You just need to interrupt the rush.

Choosing Your Pace

When you feel uncertain, the instinct is to speed up:

- Speak too quickly
- Rush your opening
- Fill silence
- Try to "fix" discomfort with words

Confident salespeople do the opposite. They pause before speaking, they let their first sentence land, then they move at a pace that communicates safety rather than urgency. Your pace influences the customer's pace. When you slow down, they slow down. When you stay steady, they open up. Pace is confidence made visible.

Letting Go of the Need to Impress

One of the biggest sources of pre-interaction anxiety is the belief:

"I need to impress this customer."

That belief creates pressure. Pressure creates tension. Tension pulls your attention inward. Confident salespeople are not trying to impress anyone. They are focused on understanding, guiding, and responding clearly. When you stop trying to perform, your presence improves naturally. Confidence is not performance. Confidence is steadiness.

A Professional Mindset Shift: "I'm the Calm One in the Room"

Here is a mindset that changes everything:

I don't need the customer to be calm. I need me to be calm.

You become the emotional stabiliser in the interaction. The customer can be nervous, sceptical, rushed, irritated, or distracted you remain steady.

Your confidence stops depending on their behaviour. You take responsibility only for what you can control: your presence.

That is professional confidence.

What This Looks Like in Practice

Right before the interaction:

- You notice your mind racing and don't fight it
- You take one slow breath
- You set one clear intention
- You consciously slow your pace
- You let go of the need to impress.

That's it. Sometimes this takes thirty seconds. Sometimes less. But it shifts you from reactive to responsive, from scattered to grounded.

The Cumulative Effect

At first, this steadiness feels deliberate. Over time, it becomes natural. You still feel nerves.
You still face uncertainty, but those feelings stop dictating your behaviour. That's when confidence becomes reliable rather than fragile something you can access regardless of mood, pressure, or difficulty.

Where We Go Next

Now that you know how to steady yourself before the interaction, **Chapter 4** takes you inside your inner voice the self-talk that either supports your confidence or quietly undermines it between conversations. Because what you say to yourself in the gaps matters just as much as what you say to customers.

Understanding Your Self-Talk

Where It Comes From and How to Take Back Control

If confidence has a voice, doubt does too. Most salespeople hear that second voice more often than they admit. It's the quiet commentary running underneath the day. The thoughts that appear before a difficult customer. The internal questioning after a flat conversation. The subtle tension that shows up when the stakes feel higher than usual. That voice is your self-talk.

It isn't dramatic. It doesn't announce itself. It simply comments warning, questioning, preparing you for what *might* go wrong. And depending on how you relate to it, that voice can either steady you or slowly undermine your confidence.

Most people try to silence it. Some try to overpower it with positivity. Others push through and hope it quietens down with experience. Confident professionals do something different.

They understand what that voice is, why it behaves the way it does, and how to lead it rather than be led by it. Before you can change your self-talk, you need to understand it properly.

What That Voice Is Actually Doing

Your inner commentary is not random. It is not weakness. And it is not proof that you "lack confidence". It is your brain doing one of its oldest jobs: trying to keep you safe.

Long before sales existed, your nervous system evolved to protect you from social risk. Being rejected, excluded, embarrassed, or seen as incompetent once carried real consequences. So, the brain developed a habit of scanning for danger and preparing for the worst.

That system is still running. When you meet a customer, your brain doesn't calmly assess the situation and conclude that everything is fine. It treats uncertainty and evaluation as potential threats and responds accordingly. It asks questions like:

- What if this goes badly?
- What if I get this wrong?
- What if I'm judged?

The problem isn't that this voice exists. The problem is that it hasn't updated its threat model for modern professional life. It reacts to customers as if they are risks to your safety rather than people making decisions.

Once you see that, something shifts. You stop arguing with the voice. You stop treating it as an enemy. You start interpreting it correctly as a protective system doing its best with outdated information.

Where the Tone of That Voice Comes From

The way you speak to yourself didn't begin in sales. It was shaped much earlier by the environments you grew up in, the people who corrected you, the way mistakes were handled, and the tone used when expectations weren't met.

Some people grow up with calm guidance. Others grow up around criticism, unpredictability, or pressure. Your brain absorbs those patterns and turns them inward. Over time, it learns a tone and adopts it as your internal voice.

That's why, under pressure, some people hear a steady, measured inner dialogue while others hear something harsher and more urgent. It isn't personality. It's conditioning.

Workplaces reinforce this further. Managers who micromanage, environments where feedback only appears when something goes wrong, cultures where targets dominate conversations all of this trains your inner voice to stay alert for criticism.

Sales amplifies these patterns because you are constantly exposed to judgement. Often from people you've never met before and from sales managers on occasions. So, when your self-talk gets louder in sales, it isn't because something is wrong with you. It's because the role repeatedly triggers systems that were designed to react to evaluation.

Why Sales Makes the Voice Louder

Selling reliably activates two psychological triggers: uncertainty and assessment. Every interaction carries both. You don't know how the conversation will go, and you know you're being evaluated sometimes openly, often silently.

Your mind responds by trying to prepare you. It runs scenarios. It highlights risks. It reminds you what could go wrong. It doesn't do this to undermine you. It does it because that's how it learned to protect you.

Unfortunately, protection and performance are not the same thing. Left unchecked, that protective voice becomes cautious, defensive, and self-critical. It consumes energy. It tightens your communication. It pulls your attention inward at exactly the moment it needs to be outward.

This is why even capable, experienced salespeople can feel mentally tired before the interaction has even begun. They've already lived through several imagined failures in their head.

The Two Voices You'll Notice Over Time

With awareness, most salespeople begin to notice something important. There isn't just one inner voice. There are two.

The first is the protective voice. Its language is urgent and cautious. It warns. It questions. It tries to keep you from making mistakes or being exposed.

The second voice is quieter, steadier, and more deliberate. It doesn't try to eliminate risk. It focuses on clarity and composure. It sounds less like anxiety and more like a good manager: calm, direct, practical.

Confident salespeople don't silence the protective voice. They hear it and then they choose to lead from the second. That distinction matters. Confidence isn't about eliminating doubt. It's about not allowing doubt to take control of your behaviour.

Why "Just Think Positive" Fails

You may have been told to ignore negative thoughts, replace them with positive ones, or block them out altogether. That advice rarely works. The mind does not respond well to suppression.

When you try to force thoughts away, you keep them active by monitoring whether they are still there. The effort creates tension, not relief. Self-talk cannot be switched off. It must be led. Real confidence is not the absence of critical thoughts. It is the ability to hear them without treating them as instructions.

The Shift That Creates Space

One of the most effective changes you can make is deceptively simple. Instead of treating thoughts as facts, you learn to notice them as mental events.

"I'm not sure I can handle this" becomes *"I'm having the thought that I might not handle this well."*

That small shift creates distance. You are no longer inside the thought. You are observing it.

This doesn't eliminate the voice, but it reduces its authority. You gain room to choose how you respond rather than reacting automatically. That space is where leadership begins.

What Professional Self-Talk Sounds Like

Professional self-talk is not loud, motivational, or dramatic. It sounds measured, it sounds grounded, it sounds like someone you trust, and it gives guidance rather than criticism. It focuses on behaviour rather than identity. It doesn't demand confidence it supports steadiness.

When salespeople talk to themselves this way, their presence changes. They slow down. They listen better, they stop trying to impress, they respond rather than defend. This is not about optimism. It's about clarity.

A Well-Led Mind, Not a Silent One

Your inner voice will always be there, it should be, its job is awareness, not control. Confidence grows as you learn to direct your attention, soften your internal pace, and choose calmer interpretations before reacting. This isn't personality-based. It's a skill that strengthens with use.

When you stop fighting your self-talk and start leading it, pressure eases. Hesitation softens. Difficult customers feel less threatening. Mistakes feel less personal. Conversations become easier because more of your attention is where it belongs with the customer.

Where This Takes Us Next

Understanding your self-talk is the foundation. Practice is what makes it reliable. In **Chapter 5**, we move into the practical tools simple, repeatable techniques that help you regulate your pace, calm your system, and reinforce professional self-talk in real situations. Understanding changes perspective. Practice builds confidence you can rely on.

Planning, Preparation, and Mental Rehearsal

How Professionals Build Confidence Before the Customer Arrives

Most salespeople walk into their day hoping confidence will show up. Professionals walk into their day having already built it. The difference isn't talent, personality, or experience. It's preparation not of scripts or product sheets, but of mindset, pacing, and expectation. The kind of preparation that keeps you steady when the day becomes unpredictable.

Up to now, this book has focused on how confidence works internally how the mind responds to uncertainty, how pressure shows up, and how to stabilise yourself in the moment. This chapter moves outward. It looks at how confident professionals prepare *before* the customer arrives, so confidence doesn't have to be manufactured under pressure. Confidence is not something you wait for. It's something you create.

Why Preparation Builds Confidence

Preparation builds confidence for three simple psychological reasons.

First, it reduces unnecessary uncertainty. The brain reacts badly to unpredictability. When you remove even a small amount of uncertainty, anxiety drops and thinking sharpens.

Second, it primes recognition. A prepared brain recognises patterns more quickly. Recognition creates familiarity. Familiarity reduces threat. Reduced threat creates calm.

Third, it lowers cognitive load. Confidence collapses when the mind is overloaded. Preparation frees mental bandwidth so you can listen, respond, and stay present instead of scrambling.

Preparation isn't for weak performers. It's what strong performers do to make their capability visible.

The Three Levels of Preparation That Matter

Most salespeople prepare but only at one level. Professionals prepare at three. These layers work together. Miss one, and confidence becomes fragile.

Level One: Technical Preparation

Product, Process, and Practicalities

This is the foundation. Knowing your product. Understanding pricing and trade-offs. Being clear on process, lead times, and constraints. Knowing where flexibility exists and where it doesn't. The psychological impact here is simple: uncertainty in knowledge creates hesitation in behaviour, and hesitation leaks confidence.

Ask yourself:

- Where do I hesitate when explaining options?
- Which questions still catch me off guard?
- What part of our process feels clumsy when I talk about it?

Anywhere you hesitate internally, customers feel it externally. But technical preparation alone does not create confidence. If it did, the most confident people in the world would all be engineers. This level removes friction it doesn't yet create steadiness.

Level Two: Situational Preparation

Preparing for the Day You're Actually Going to Have

Most salespeople prepare for product questions. Professionals prepare for situations. Situational preparation means anticipating:

- The types of customers you're likely to meet
- The objections that reliably appear
- The emotional states people arrive in
- The points in the process where conversations wobble

If you work in any repeat environment automotive, property, finance, holidays, B2B services patterns repeat daily. High performers don't treat those patterns as surprises. They ask themselves, quietly and realistically:

- Who am I likely to meet today?
- What objections am I almost guaranteed to hear?
- Where do conversations usually tighten or stall?
- What moments typically test my patience or confidence?

When you walk into known territory, your system relaxes. Control increases. Confidence follows. But there's still a third layer and this is the one that separates experienced from exceptional.

Level Three: Psychological Preparation

The Difference Between Feeling Ready and Being Ready

This layer is rarely taught, and it changes everything. Psychological preparation is not about imagining success. It's about rehearsing professionalism.

It means preparing:

- How you want to show up
- The pace you want to hold
- How you respond when challenged
- How you reset if things wobble
- How you sound when you're calm and grounded

Your brain responds to mental rehearsal almost as strongly as real experience. When you mentally preview realistic situations not fantasy, but likely difficulty your nervous system recognises the pattern when it appears. Recognition reduces threat, reduced threat allows confidence.

This is why elite performers in every field rehearse mentally. Not to perfect performance, but to stabilise state.

What Five Minutes of Real Preparation Looks Like

This isn't a ritual. It isn't motivational. It doesn't require silence or breathing exercises.

It looks like this:

You briefly name the day you're likely to have busy, quiet, mixed, challenging. Naming it calibrates your system.

You mentally walk through one or two *likely* difficult interactions. Not perfectly. Realistically, a hesitant buyer, a price challenge. Someone carrying frustration from elsewhere. You picture yourself staying steady.

You choose one good question you'll ask today. Just one. Confidence grows through simplicity.

You decide the tone you'll hold calm, curious, professional not excited, not urgent.

You commit to your pace. If you rush, confidence leaks. If you hold pace, control returns.

That's it.

Five minutes or less. But it changes how you enter the day.

Preparing for the Objections You Already Know Are Coming

Every industry has the same handful of objections on repeat:

- Price
- Timing
- Comparison
- Trust
- Uncertainty

Most salespeople know this but still get thrown, because they haven't prepared psychologically for how they want to respond. A simple discipline makes a disproportionate difference. Write down the five objections you hear most often.

For each, note:

- That the customer usually means
- That they're worried about
- That they need to hear to relax
- Your best steady response

Not clever. Not scripted. Just calm, grounded professionalism. When you've already decided how you'll respond, you don't wobble when the moment arrives. This is the difference between experience and reliability.

The Confidence Buffer

Preparation creates a buffer. A margin of emotional stability that protects you when:

- The day starts slowly
- Customers appear to be difficult
- Questions come from nowhere
- Rejection lands harder than usual
- Energy dips or pressure rises

Unprepared salespeople rely on momentum. When momentum fades, so does confidence. Prepared salespeople carry reserves. They built confidence before the chaos started, so they're responding not scrambling. That's why some people still feel steady at four o'clock while others are exhausted by eleven.

What Customers Actually Notice

Customers never see your preparation, but they feel the results.

- Your voice is calmer
- Your explanations are clearer
- You pause rather than rush
- You handle tension without defensiveness
- You ask better questions
- You stay composed when challenged

Preparation is invisible but its effects are unmistakable. Professionals aren't confident because things go well. Things go well because professionals are confident.

Bringing It Together

Confidence is not created in the moment of pressure. It's created before pressure arrives. When you prepare *technically*, *situationally*, and *psychologically*, you stop hoping confidence will appear and start arriving with it already in place. This doesn't make days easy. It makes them manageable and that's what real confidence looks like.

Where We Go Next

Preparation gets you into the room steady. In **Chapter 6**, we deal with what happens *inside* the interaction when customers challenge you, hesitate, push back, or apply pressure. Because confidence isn't just about entering calmly. It's about staying composed when it's tested.

CHAPTER 6:

Handling Pressure in the Moment

How to Stay Composed, Clear, and in Control When It Matters Most

Pressure doesn't arrive politely in sales. It shows up suddenly in a price challenge, a comparison, a stretch of silence, a sharp question, or a confrontational remark you weren't expecting. One moment the conversation is flowing. The next, your body tightens and your mind accelerates.

Most salespeople experience that moment the same way: pressure hits, and they instinctively try to do *more*.

- They talk faster
- They explain harder
- They fill silence
- They justify
- They convince

And almost every time, it makes things worse. Confident professionals do something that looks deceptively simple from the outside. When pressure arrives, they do **less**, not more and that single shift changes the entire interaction.

What Pressure Actually Does to You

When a customer challenges you, doubts you, or hesitates, your nervous system reacts before you've consciously chosen a response. This isn't weakness. It's automatic. Pressure triggers a social threat response the possibility of being judged, rejected, or seen as incompetent. Your system mobilises. It speeds you up. It pushes you toward action. It urges you to *fix* the situation quickly.

That response makes sense in physical danger. In conversation, it's exactly the wrong move. Acceleration reads as anxiety. Over-explaining reads as uncertainty. Filling silence reads as lack of confidence. Customers don't analyse this intellectually. They feel it. The key skill in this chapter is not eliminating that reaction it's interrupting it.

The First Behaviour: Slow Down When Everything Tells You to Speed Up

Watch confident professionals under pressure and you'll notice something subtle. They pause. Not dramatically. Not awkwardly. Just long enough to stop reacting. A half-second beat between challenge and response does two things at once:

- Internally, it interrupts the automatic stress response and gives you choice back
- Externally, it signals thoughtfulness and composure.

A customer says, *"That's more than I was expecting."* Instead of launching into justification, the professional pauses.

That pause says: *I've heard you. I'm not threatened. I'm thinking.*

This is where confidence lives in the space between stimulus and response.

The Second Behaviour: Ask Before You Explain

Under pressure, most salespeople explain. Professionals ask. Questions buy time without looking like avoidance. They gather information instead of guessing. They slow the customer down and move the conversation from reaction to reflection. We speak around 120-200 words per minute, yet we think at around 2,000 words per minute, so asking a question and listening to their answer gives you more thinking time, which increases confidence as we start to uncover the unknown.

Simple questions do the heaviest lifting:

- "What were you expecting?"
- "Tell me more about that."
- "What's the main concern here?"
- "What are you comparing this to?"

These aren't clever techniques. They're composure in action. When you ask a question, you stop defending and start understanding. The dynamic shifts from *me versus you* to *us looking at this together*. Pressure eases because the problem becomes clearer.

The Third Behaviour: Say One Thing Then Stop

Pressure makes your mind want to say everything. Every reason, every justification, every possible angle that might convince. Confident professionals resist that urge, they say **one clear thing**, then they stop.

- One point
- One explanation
- One clarification

Then silence, silence is not a failure of confidence. It's evidence of it. If what you've said is enough, the customer will respond. If it isn't, they'll tell you what they still need. Long explanations under pressure don't sound thorough. They sound uncertain. If your response wouldn't fit on a sticky note, it's probably too much.

The Fourth Behaviour: Hold Your Tone, Not Just Your Words

In pressured moments, customers aren't primarily listening to *what* you say. They're responding to *how* you say it. Tone carries more weight than logic when emotions are involved. A calm tone with an imperfect answer beats a perfect answer delivered with tension.

Confident professionals instinctively regulate three things:

- They slow their speech slightly
- They lower their volume
- They soften urgency in their delivery

This isn't manipulation. It's self-regulation. When you slow your voice, your thinking slows with it. When you lower your volume, the customer leans in rather than pulling back. When urgency drops, trust rises. Customers feel steadiness before they understand content.

When Confidence Wobbles Mid-Conversation

Even experienced salespeople feel moments where confidence slips. You notice your shoulders tighten, your pace creeps up, your thoughts scatter. The difference is not that professionals never wobble it's that they have a way to reset *inside* the moment.

Most use a simple internal phrase:

- "Slow down."
- "Stay curious."
- "One thing at a time."

Not motivational. Not dramatic. Just enough to interrupt the spiral and return to presence.

A brief pause, one breath, a quieter voice. The conversation doesn't need to stop; you just need to come back to centre.

What Customers Actually Experience When You Do This

When you slow down, ask questions, say less, and hold your tone, customers don't consciously label you as confident. They feel something more important, they feel safe.

Safe enough to explain their concern, safe enough to admit hesitation, safe enough to be honest about money, fear, or uncertainty.

That sense of safety doesn't come from perfect technique. It comes from your ability to stay composed when things are uncomfortable and that is what trust is built on.

Bringing It Together

Pressure is unavoidable in sales. Confidence isn't about avoiding it it's about responding differently when it arrives.

When pressure hits:

- Pause instead of rushing
- Ask instead of explaining
- Say one thing instead of many
- Hold your tone
- Reset when needed

These behaviours are simple, that's why they work. They don't depend on personality, they don't require scripts, they don't collapse under stress. They are ways of *being*, not tricks and they can be practiced until they become automatic.

Where We Go Next

Handling pressure in the moment is only half the challenge. In **Chapter 7**, we look at what happens *after* the interaction when customers say no, disappear, delay, or leave you with unanswered questions. Because unmanaged rejection doesn't just affect confidence once. It accumulates and learning how to process it properly is what keeps confidence intact over time.

Handling Rejection Without Losing Confidence

How to Stay Motivated, Professional, and Grounded When Customers Say "No"

Confidence isn't tested when things go well. It's tested when pressure appears. The next chapters deal with the moments that quietly erode confidence if you don't know how to handle them.

Rejection hurts even when you're experienced, even when you're professional, even when you know it's "part of the job". Anyone who tells you to simply *shake it off* or *not take it personally* has never really thought about what rejection does to the human system. Rejection lands because you care about doing your job well and being seen accurately. That isn't weakness. It's humanity.

What damages confidence isn't rejection itself. It's what happens after when rejection is misunderstood, mislabelled, and allowed to accumulate. This chapter is about preventing that damage.

Why Rejection Feels Sharper in Sales

Sales places you in a repeated cycle of approach and outcome. You step forward. You engage. You invest attention and effort and sometimes the answer is simply "no". That "no" can activate three deep human sensitivities at once:

First, the need for acceptance. Being dismissed or declined triggers the same neural pathways as physical pain. Your system reacts before logic has time to catch up.

Second, the need to feel competent. Even when you know intellectually that rejection isn't personal, the emotional system can still translate "no" into "I failed".

Third, the need for predictability. Rejection interrupts rhythm. A good morning can suddenly feel derailed by a single interaction.

This is why even capable, professional salespeople can feel an abrupt drop in energy after rejection deflated, frustrated, self-critical, or simply tired. Nothing unusual is happening. This is a normal human response to uncertainty and evaluation.

The Biggest Misunderstanding About Rejection

Most confidence damage in sales comes from a single misunderstanding.

Rejection is rarely about:

- Your skill
- Your professionalism
- Your personality
- Your value
- Your worth

Yet many salespeople interpret it that way.

In reality, people say no because:

- Timing is wrong
- Budgets are constrained
- They don't trust their own decision yet
- They're comparing options

- Someone else influences the decision
- They feel overwhelmed
- They're risk-averse by nature

You are one variable in a complex psychological and practical equation. When rejection is misinterpreted as personal feedback, confidence erodes. When rejection is understood correctly, it becomes information not identity.

The Three Types of Rejection

Professionals protect their confidence by recognising *what kind* of rejection they're dealing with. There are only three.

Situational rejection is the most common.
"Not now."
"Not today."
"I need to think."

This is about timing, circumstance, or competing priorities. Once you recognise it for what it is, it carries very little emotional weight.

Product or offer rejection is about fit.
"It's not right for me."
"I'm not sure this suits what we need."

This is not a judgement of you. It's a mismatch and professionals accept mismatches calmly.

Personal mismatch rejection is rare.

It usually involves a customer who is stressed, defensive, angry, or mistrustful and you happen to be the person in front of them. Even here, the emotion is situational. It's aimed *through* you, not *at* you. Confidence stays intact when rejection is categorised correctly instead of absorbed emotionally.

The Real Damage: Rejection Hangover

The rejection itself is rarely the problem. The problem is what follows. A dip in energy, a subtle change in your tone, a quicker pace and harsher self-talk. A slightly diminished version of you meeting the next customer.

This is rejection hangover and it costs more sales than rejection ever does. Unprocessed rejection carries forward. It quietly shapes the rest of the day. And customers feel it, even if they don't know why. The goal is not to avoid rejection. The goal is to stop it *lingering*.

The Six-Second Reset

Professionals use a simple reset immediately after rejection not to feel better, but to prevent emotional distortion. It takes seconds.

First, **exhale deliberately**. Rejection triggers a small adrenaline spike. A conscious breath out helps switch off the internal alarm.

Second, **label the rejection accurately**:

"This was situational, not personal."
"That was their story, not mine."
"Timing, not failure."

This stops your brain from writing the wrong narrative.

Third, **reset your body**. Straighten posture. Drop your shoulders. Slow your movement. Physiology leads psychology.

Fourth, **reset your identity** with one quiet sentence:
"I'm still the professional here."

That sentence matters more than it looks. It prevents a single outcome from rewriting who you believe yourself to be. If you do nothing, rejection processes *you*. If you do this, you process it and move on cleanly.

The Ratio Mindset

Here is one of the most protective shifts a salesperson can make. Professionals treat rejection mathematically, not emotionally. If your average close ratio is three-to-one, then every "no" is expected. It's not failure. It's movement through the numbers.

Amateurs experience rejection as a judgement. Professionals experience it as progress. Your job isn't to win every conversation. Your job is to stay intact long enough to reach the next "yes".

Filtering Rejection Instead of Absorbing It

When rejection occurs, professionals instinctively sort it:

Is this a **timing issue** something to follow up later?
A **fit issue** something to reposition or redirect?
An **information issue** something to clarify?
An **emotional issue** something to disengage from cleanly?

This mental filter transforms rejection from something you *feel* into something you *understand*. Clarity replaces rumination. Confidence stabilises.

Separating Self-Worth From Outcomes

This distinction is non-negotiable for long-term confidence. Sales outcomes measure activity and circumstance not worth. You can perform well and still lose a sale. You can perform poorly and still get lucky. Outcomes fluctuate. Professional behaviour doesn't.

When confidence is based on:

- Preparation
- Behaviour
- Consistency
- Professionalism

It becomes resilient. When confidence is based on customer decisions, it becomes fragile.

Recovering From a Tough Run

Everyone experiences runs of rejection. Professionals recover by applying three principles:

1. They keep a **short emotional memory** retaining lessons, not feelings.
2. They maintain **high behavioural standards** posture, tone, pace.
3. They deliberately **slow down**, preventing spirals.

Each customer deserves a fresh version of you. The previous customer's decision does not get to set the tone, you do.

The Reframe That Changes Everything

Here is the reframe that quietly transforms daily experience: Rejection is not proof that something is wrong. It is proof that you are active. The only people who avoid rejection are those who avoid effort.

"No's", delays, objections, and difficult customers mean you are in the arena engaging, working, and stretching. Avoiding rejection is a sign of underperformance. Experiencing it is a sign of participation. Handled properly, rejection doesn't weaken confidence. It strengthens it.

What Customers Notice

Customers notice how you carry yourself after a "no". They notice composure, they notice professionalism, they notice steadiness rather than desperation. Rejection is a test most salespeople don't realise they're taking. Handle it well, and credibility rises. Trust deepens. You become memorable for the right reasons.

Where We Go Next

Pressure and rejection are external challenges. In **Chapter 8**, we turn to quieter ones slow days, empty periods, lost momentum, and the confidence dip that comes when nothing seems to be happening. Because confidence isn't only tested when things go wrong. It's tested when nothing happens at all.

Managing Quiet Days Without Losing Momentum

Why Low Activity Is Risky and How Professionals Stay in Control

Quiet days are more dangerous to confidence than bad ones. On a difficult day, you're engaged, you're responding, you're involved. Even rejection has shape and energy. Something is happening. On a quiet day, nothing pushes back.

- No customers
- No objections
- No decisions
- No momentum

And without realising it, confidence begins to leak not through failure, but through drift. This chapter is about recognising that risk early and managing yourself deliberately when activity drops. Not with frantic busyness, but with calm, purposeful control.

What Actually Happens on Quiet Days

When sales activity slows, the external structure of the day disappears. There's less urgency, fewer interruptions, more empty space. That space is not neutral. Without pressure to respond outwardly, attention turns inward. The mind fills gaps with speculation, comparison, and self-evaluation. You start replaying previous conversations. You wonder whether things are going as well as they should. You begin measuring yourself against imagined standards. Nothing has gone wrong, but confidence starts to thin. This isn't laziness. It's human psychology responding to a lack of stimulus. Quiet removes friction, and friction is often what keeps people focused.

The Drift (And Why It's So Subtle)

The real danger of quiet days is not inactivity. It's drift.

- Drift looks like:
- Lower posture
- Softer pace
- Less precision in language
- Lower expectations of yourself
- Mild disengagement disguised as "waiting"

You don't notice it happening, but customers do. When the next interaction finally arrives, you're slightly underpowered not unprofessional, just not fully present. Confidence hasn't collapsed. It has *thinned*. Professionals understand this pattern. They don't wait for activity to restore energy. They take responsibility for maintaining it.

Why "Just Relax" Is the Wrong Advice

Quiet days often come with well-meaning advice:

- "Enjoy it."
- "Use the time to relax."
- "It'll pick up again."

Relaxation isn't the problem. Loss of structure is. Confidence thrives on rhythm. When rhythm disappears, confidence needs *replacement structure* not pressure, not hustle, but deliberate engagement. Professionals don't panic on quiet days, but they don't surrender control either.

The Rule Professionals Live By: Activity Creates Confidence

Confidence does not come from results alone. It comes from forward motion. Action restores identity. It reminds you that you are active, capable, and engaged regardless of whether customers are currently responding.

The mistake many salespeople make is tying confidence to outcome. When outcomes slow, confidence fades. Professionals tie confidence to behaviour. You cannot control when customers arrive. You can control how you carry yourself while waiting.

Choosing Productive Action (Not Busywork)

This is not about filling time. It's about choosing actions that reinforce professionalism.

On quiet days, professionals deliberately do things that:

- Sharpen clarity
- Reinforce competence
- Keep posture high
- Preserve momentum

That might mean:

- Reviewing recent conversations for learning, not judgement
- Refining how you explain one key option or trade-off
- Preparing for the *next* objection you know will come
- Following up cleanly, even when you expect nothing back
- Resetting your physical environment or workspace
- Rehearsing calm responses, not pitches

The purpose isn't productivity. The purpose is *identity maintenance*.

The "Next Person Wins" Mindset

Quiet days tempt you to attach emotional weight to the *last* interaction. Professionals focus on the next. Not with false optimism but with discipline. Every new customer deserves a full-strength version of you. Not the residue of boredom, frustration, or overthinking. The next person wins because you decide they do. This mindset prevents confidence from being held hostage by timing.

Zooming Out Without Disconnecting

Another quiet-day trap is overthinking the big picture. You start questioning the week, then the month, then your performance, then your future. Perspective matters but timing matters too. Professionals zoom out briefly, then return to the present. They ask:

- "Is this a normal fluctuation?"
- "What's actually in my control today?"
- "What behaviour would I respect if I saw someone else doing it right now?"

They don't spiral. They recalibrate.

Maintaining Professional Standards When No One Is Watching

Quiet days reveal something important. Not how well you sell but how well you lead yourself.

- Posture
- Tone
- Pace
- Attention

These things are easiest to let slip when there's no immediate consequence. Professionals maintain standards anyway not for appearance, but for internal consistency. Confidence is built when your behaviour matches your identity, even in empty moments.

The Quiet Discipline That Preserves Confidence

Here is the discipline that separates professionals from everyone else:

They treat quiet days as active responsibility, not passive waiting.

They don't rush.
They don't drift.
They don't disengage.

They stay ready.

Not tense, not forced, just prepared. That steadiness accumulates. And when activity returns as it always does confidence is intact.

Bringing It Together

Quiet days don't announce themselves as dangerous. They feel harmless, they feel uneventful, they feel easy. That's why they matter. Confidence is not only tested when things go wrong. It's tested when nothing happens. Professionals don't wait for momentum. They *maintain it*.

Where We Go Next

So far, we've dealt with:

- Pressure
- Rejection
- Inactivity

In **Chapter 9**, we turn to something more subtle again: consistency. Because confidence isn't built in peaks. It's built in how reliably you show up over time.

Managing End-of-Season Fatigue

How to Stay Effective, Energised, and Confident When Your Tank Is Running Low

There comes a point in every sales cycle when something quietly changes. You're still showing up, you're still doing the job, you're still professional. But the work feels heavier than it used to. The conversations blur together. Your patience shortens. Objections land harder. Even straightforward interactions take more effort than they should. Nothing dramatic has gone wrong and that's what makes it difficult to name.

This is end-of-season fatigue. And it affects even the most capable salespeople.

Martin's Story-A Familiar Pattern

In October 2019, I received a call from a sales manager at a caravan park in North Wales. "Can you come and take a look at one of my team?" he asked. "He's one of our best people, but something's off."

When I arrived the following Tuesday, the numbers told a familiar story. Strong performance through spring. Excellent results through summer. A gradual dip in September. And now, in October, something that felt less like fluctuation and more like depletion.

The salesperson I'll call him Martin had been with the business for eight years. Reliable. Well-liked. Consistently solid.

"He's not doing anything obviously wrong," the manager said. "He's here on time. He's professional. He's talking to customers. But the energy's gone. It's like he's running on empty."

I spent the day observing Martin. Nothing was broken but everything was slightly off. He greeted customers politely, but without the natural warmth he once had. His explanations were accurate, but they took effort. When objections appeared, he handled them, but you could see the internal cost. By mid-afternoon, he looked exhausted in a way that had nothing to do with sleep.

At the end of the day, I sat down with him. "How are you feeling about work at the moment?" I asked. He paused for a long moment. "Honestly?" he said. "I'm done. Not quitting done just… empty. Every customer feels like work. I used to enjoy this job. Right now, I'm just getting through days." Martin wasn't underperforming. He was depleted.

What Fatigue Really Is

Sales fatigue is rarely about effort in a single moment. It's about accumulation. Sales isn't just the act of selling. It's the repeated exposure to:

- Uncertainty
- Scrutiny
- Emotional regulation
- Objections
- Rejection
- Decision pressure
- Other people's stress

Each interaction on its own is manageable. Over months, they compound. Martin had been carrying that load since early spring. Summer had been intense back-to-back customers, quick decisions, constant engagement.

There was no recovery time between interactions. Every difficult moment was followed immediately by another customer.

By the time autumn arrived and the pace slowed, the busyness that had been masking his fatigue disappeared. What was left was depletion. "I thought I was just losing my edge," Martin said. "Like maybe I wasn't as good as I used to be."

That misinterpretation is where confidence really starts to erode.

The Two Faces of End-of-Season Fatigue

Fatigue shows up differently depending on where you are in the cycle.

In busy periods, fatigue comes from overload:

- Constant stimulation
- No recovery between customers
- Decision fatigue
- Emotional compression

In quieter periods, fatigue comes from under-stimulation:

- Loss of rhythm
- Too much internal space
- Self-evaluation creeping in
- Identity wobble

Both drain confidence just in different ways. Martin experienced both. Summer exhausted him through intensity. Autumn drained him through silence. By October, he was trying to operate at full capacity with no reserves left.

The Moment It Clicked

I asked Martin a simple question. "What would you look like if you were at your best right now?" He didn't hesitate. "I'd be calmer. Sharper. More present. I'd have patience again." "And what's actually happening?" "I'm going through the motions. I know what to say, but it feels mechanical." "You're not worse at your job," I said. "You're tired. Those are different problems." That distinction mattered. Fatigue had been masquerading as decline.

What Professionals Do Differently

Most salespeople try to *push through* end-of-season fatigue. Professionals manage it.

They don't rely on motivation or adrenaline. They rely on:

- Pacing
- Micro-recovery
- State control
- Behavioural standards

The goal isn't to feel energised. It's to stay effective.

Small Changes That Restore Capacity

We focused on a few deliberate shifts.

Pace came first.

Fatigue makes people rush. Rushing increases error and stress. Martin slowed himself down by ten percent speech, movement, breathing. That alone restored presence.

Then micro-recovery.

Every ninety minutes, he stepped away briefly. Two minutes. No phone. Shoulders back. Slow breath. Reset posture. These tiny resets stopped fatigue from accumulating unchecked.

Then freshness per interaction.

Before each customer, he asked himself: *"How would I handle this if it were my first customer of the day?"* Not to generate energy but to concentrate it.

Finally, letting go.

Each evening, he deliberately released the day: *What doesn't need to come with me tomorrow?* Within a week, his sleep improved. Within weeks, his confidence returned.

Six Weeks Later

I checked in with Martin near the end of the season. "How's it going?" I asked. "Better than summer," he said. "I'm not as busy but I'm present again." His close rate had recovered. More importantly, so had his enjoyment of the work. "I didn't need to try harder," he said. "I needed to stop draining myself without noticing."

The Bigger Pattern

Martin's story isn't unusual. I see it in estate agents in late autumn. Car sales teams at year-end. Financial advisors at the end of tax cycles. B2B teams after long project pushes. The people who finish strong aren't tougher. They're more self-managed. They understand that confidence fades quietly when fatigue is ignored and they intervene early.

Bringing It Together

End-of-season fatigue is not a failure of resilience. It's the predictable result of sustained emotional output without deliberate recovery. Confidence isn't lost in one bad moment. It thins gradually when reserves run low. When you manage pace, recovery, and standards deliberately, confidence holds even when energy dips. That's how professionals finish seasons strong.

Where We Go Next

Fatigue challenges stamina. The next chapter challenges composure. In **Chapter 10**, we look at how to stay calm, professional, and confident when customers themselves become difficult because tired or not, your confidence still needs to hold when people test it.

Handling Difficult Customers with Confidence

How to Stay Calm, Professional, and in Control When People Test You

Every salesperson encounters difficult customers. The ones who arrive defensive or suspicious. The ones who challenge aggressively or interrupt constantly. The ones who seem irritated before the conversation even starts. They exist in every industry, at every price point, in every market. And dealing with them drains confidence faster than almost anything else not because they are hard to satisfy, but because they test your composure.

The most important thing to understand is this: A difficult customer is rarely a reflection of your ability. They are a reflection of their state.

Their behaviour is almost always shaped by:

- Stress
- Fear of making a bad decision
- Financial pressure
- Previous negative experiences
- Lack of trust in the buying process
- Frustration carried in from elsewhere

If you take that behaviour personally, confidence collapses. If you understand it correctly, confidence holds. This chapter is about recognising difficult patterns early and staying grounded, professional, and in control regardless of who is in front of you.

Why Difficult Customers Shake Confidence So Quickly

Difficult customers feel threatening because they trigger three deeply wired responses at once.

First, a **threat response**.

A sharp tone or confrontational stance is interpreted by the nervous system as danger. Your body prepares to defend itself.

Second, a **status challenge**.
When a customer asserts dominance or superiority, it can quietly undermine your sense of authority if you're not anchored.

Third, an **emotional ambush**.
You weren't expecting hostility, so the suddenness throws you off balance. None of this is weakness. It's biology.

Professionals don't try to eliminate these reactions. They learn to contain them and respond deliberately rather than reflexively.

The Four Common Types of Difficult Customers

Most difficult behaviour follows predictable patterns. Recognising the pattern removes much of the emotional shock. These are not labels they are temporary states, and customers often move between them.

1. The Defensive Customer

This customer arrives guarded emotionally, sometimes physically. They are protecting themselves from pressure, embarrassment, or regret.

You'll notice:

- Short answers
- Limited warmth
- Suspicion of your intentions

This behaviour is driven by fear, not hostility.

Your job is not to push.
It's to slow the interaction down and create psychological safety. When you remain calm, curious, and unhurried, defensiveness usually softens on its own.

2. The Dominant Customer

This customer wants control. They may interrupt, challenge your statements, or speak abruptly. Not because they dislike you but because dominance helps them feel safe. If you rush, defend, or match their intensity, you lose authority. If you stay steady, grounded, and structured, authority naturally returns to you. Dominant customers don't respect force. They respect composure.

3. The Overwhelmed Customer

This customer is flooded. They may appear inconsistent, emotional, indecisive, or scattered. They aren't difficult by nature they're overloaded.

You'll hear:

- Changing priorities
- Uncertainty
- Frustration with themselves as much as the situation

Your role here is containment, not speed. When you slow the pace, reduce options, and guide step by step, overwhelm reduces. Confidence is built through clarity, not persuasion.

4. The Distrustful Customer

This customer has been burned before. Their tone may be sharp. Their questions may feel probing or cynical. Warmth is minimal. This behaviour isn't aimed at you personally it's aimed at the process. Trust is rebuilt through consistency, transparency, and steadiness. Not through reassurance, not through over-explaining. Distrust softens when the customer senses professionalism rather than persuasion.

Your First Responsibility: Don't Absorb Their State

Difficult customers are not dangerous. They are dysregulated. If you absorb their state, you'll notice yourself:

- Rushing
- Defending
- Talking too much
- Matching their tension
- Losing pace
- Losing presence

The first rule with difficult customers is simple: Do not join their emotional state. Hold yours.

Your calm becomes the stabilising force in the conversation.

The Core Skill: Containment

Containment is the ability to keep someone else's emotional intensity within the boundaries of professionalism, without letting it leak into your own state.

It shows up as:

A calm, even tone

A slower pace

Grounded posture

Minimal reactivity

Clear structure

You acknowledge without agreeing. You hear without absorbing. For example:

Customer: "You people always try to push the most expensive option."

You: "I hear that this hasn't always been a positive process for you. Let's slow things down and look at what actually fits."

No defensiveness. No argument. Just containment.

Regaining Control Without Confrontation

When a customer is difficult, conversations often feel chaotic. Professionals restore order quietly.

They do this by asking reset questions simple questions that reintroduce structure:

- "What's the most important thing for you today?"
- "What's your biggest concern right now?"
- "What do you want to make sure we get right?"

These questions:

- Slow the interaction
- Calm the customer
- Signal professionalism
- Bring focus back to the task

Disorder fades when direction reappears.

When Boundaries Are Needed

Occasionally, behaviour crosses a line. Tone becomes disrespectful. Language becomes inappropriate. The interaction becomes unproductive. Professionals don't escalate. They reset the boundary calmly.

A simple line is enough:

"I want to help you properly, but we need to keep this respectful. Let's take it step by step."

Delivered calmly, this line is firm, fair, and authoritative. Most customers soften immediately because you handled the moment with maturity, not emotion.

Listening Beyond Words

With difficult customers, the real signal is emotional, not verbal.

- Ask yourself quietly:
- Are they anxious?
- Are they trying to protect themselves?
- Are they overwhelmed?
- Are they asserting control?
- Are they afraid of making a mistake?

Once you identify the emotional driver, behaviour becomes understandable and far easier to manage. Understanding reduces friction. Composure restores confidence.

The Real Test of Confidence

Difficult customers don't test your sales ability. They test the stability of your professionalism. Confidence grows when you realise:

- You can stay calm when someone else isn't
- You can stay polite when someone is sharp
- You can stay structured when someone is chaotic
- You can stay steady when someone is testing you

The customer's behaviour does not define your performance. Your behaviour does.

Bringing It Together

You don't need every customer to be easy. You need every version of you to be consistent. Difficult customers are part of the job. Staying grounded with them is a skill and a marker of professionalism. When you stop trying to manage people and focus instead on managing your state, confidence stops depending on who walks through the door.

Where We Go Next

Now that you can stay confident under pressure, rejection, inactivity, and difficult customers, the final step is making confidence permanent. In **Chapter 11**, we move into habits and rhythms the daily, weekly, and monthly behaviours that turn confidence from a skill you use into a professional identity you carry.

CHAPTER 11:

Confidence as a Professional Identity

What Changes When Confidence Stops Being Conditional

Up to this point, confidence has been something you manage. From here on, it becomes something you inhabit. By this point in the book, something important should already have shifted, not dramatically, not emotionally, but quietly. You should no longer be trying to feel confident. You should be starting to recognise a different way of operating calmer, steadier, more deliberate that doesn't rise and fall with customers, outcomes, or daily conditions. That shift matters, because real confidence is not a technique you apply. It's an identity you inhabit.

The Difference Between Borrowed Confidence and Built Confidence

Most salespeople operate with borrowed confidence.

It comes from:

- Good days
- Positive customers
- Quick wins
- External validation
- Momentum

Borrowed confidence feels good but it's fragile. When conditions change, it evaporates. Built confidence works differently.

It comes from:

- How you prepare
- How you regulate yourself
- How you respond under pressure
- How you handle rejection
- How you carry yourself on quiet days
- How you remain professional when others are not

Built confidence doesn't spike. It stabilises, and once it's built, it becomes yours, not something the day gives or takes away.

What Confident Professionals Have in Common

Confident professionals don't share a personality type. Some are quiet, some are direct, some are analytical and some are relational. What they share is not style its internal posture.

They:

- Don't rush to prove themselves
- Don't personalise customer behaviour
- Don't chase emotional reassurance
- Don't panic in uncertainty
- Don't carry yesterday into today

They are not detached. They are anchored. Confidence, at this level, is not about feeling strong. It's about being settled.

The Shift That Makes Confidence Permanent

Earlier in the book, we separated confidence from:

- Pressure
- Rejection
- Activity
- Customer behaviour

Now we separate it from something even more important: mood.

Professionals do not ask: "How do I feel today?"

They ask: "How do I operate, regardless?"

This doesn't mean ignoring emotion. It means not allowing emotion to dictate standards. Confidence becomes permanent when your behaviour is no longer negotiated internally each day. You don't decide whether to be steady. You are steady.

Identity Is Built Through Repetition, Not Insight

Nothing in this book works because you understand it. It works because you repeat it.

Confidence solidifies when:

- You pause instead of rush again and again
- You reset after rejection again and again
- You prepare calmly again and again
- You hold standards on quiet days again and again
- You contain pressure without reacting again and again

Eventually, there's nothing left to think about. Your nervous system learns: "This is how we do things now." That's identity.

Why This Changes How Others Experience You

When confidence becomes identity, something subtle but powerful happens. Customers stop testing you as much. Colleagues treat you differently. Difficult people soften more quickly. Silence feels less awkward. Decisions feel less charged. Not because you're doing anything clever but because you're no longer broadcasting uncertainty. You don't signal confidence. You radiate steadiness and people respond to that instinctively.

The End of Performance

One of the quiet gifts of real confidence is this:

- You stop performing
- You stop managing impressions
- You stop monitoring how you're coming across
- You stop adjusting yourself to control outcomes
- Your attention moves outward to the customer, the conversation, the moment.

Performance creates tension. Presence creates trust. This is why experienced professionals often look relaxed even in high-stakes moments. They're not "on". They're just there.

Confidence as Self-Leadership

At its core, everything in this book has been about one thing: leading yourself well. Before you lead a conversation, before you influence a decision and before you handle pressure. Confidence isn't bravado. It's self-trust.

Trust that you can:

- Stay calm
- Respond thoughtfully
- Recover cleanly
- Maintain standards
- Handle whatever comes next

When that trust is established, confidence no longer needs protecting.

What Stays With You After This Book

You will still have difficult days. You will still meet difficult people. You will still experience rejection, fatigue, and uncertainty. But you will no longer be confused by them.

You'll recognise:

- What's happening
- Why it's happening
- How to respond
- When to reset
- When to let go

That clarity is confidence. Not the loud kind. The reliable kind.

The Quiet Marker of Success

Here is how you'll know this book has done its job. Not when you feel confident.

But when:

- Pressure arrives and you don't brace
- Rejection happens and you don't carry it
- Quiet days come and you don't drift
- Difficult customers appear and you don't harden
- Uncertainty shows up and you stay present

At that point, confidence is no longer something you work on. It's simply how you work.

A Final Thought

The strongest professionals don't look confident because they've mastered sales. They look confident because they've mastered themselves. That's the work you've been doing here, and it doesn't end with this book it continues every time you choose steadiness over reaction, clarity over noise, and professionalism over performance. That choice, repeated, becomes identity.

CHAPTER 12:

Recovering from Mistakes Without Losing Confidence

Why Errors Don't Damage Confidence Self-Judgement Does

This chapter deals with recovery after specific moments go wrong. Every salesperson remembers their mistakes, not the minor ones, the ones that linger. The conversation you replay in your head on the drive home. The moment you realise you said the wrong thing. The follow-up you handled poorly. The deal you lost and can't quite explain. What makes these moments difficult isn't the error itself. It's what happens after. Confidence rarely collapses in the moment of a mistake. It collapses later in the quiet, when the internal commentary starts.

A Familiar Experience

I once worked with a senior sales consultant highly experienced, well respected, consistently strong. One afternoon, he mishandled a pricing conversation. Nothing dramatic. No shouting. No complaint. Just a subtle misjudgement of timing. The customer disengaged, and the opportunity drifted away.

By any objective measure, it was a normal sales outcome, but the impact on him was disproportionate. Over the following days, his energy dipped, his tone tightened. He second-guessed decisions he would normally make with ease. His confidence hadn't disappeared it had fractured. "I should have known better," he said. "That was amateur." That sentence did far more damage than the mistake ever did.

Why Mistakes Land So Hard

Sales mistakes cut deep because they strike at three things professionals care about.

First, **competence**.
You take pride in knowing your craft. When something goes wrong, it threatens that self-image.

Second, **reputation**.
Sales is public work. Mistakes feel visible, even when they aren't.

Third, **identity**.
Many salespeople don't just do sales they are salespeople. A mistake can feel like evidence that the identity itself is flawed. None of this is irrational, but none of it is accurate either.

The Critical Distinction Most People Miss

Here is the distinction that changes everything:

- Mistakes are information
- Self-judgement is interpretation
- Information is useful
- Interpretation is optional

Professionals review errors to learn. Amateurs replay errors to punish themselves. The difference isn't resilience. It's leadership of the inner narrative.

How Confidence Is Actually Damaged

Confidence is not damaged by making a mistake.

It is damaged by:

- Replaying it repeatedly
- Attaching meaning to it
- Questioning your ability because of it
- Allowing one moment to redefine you

This is where self-talk quietly turns corrosive.

Instead of:

"That didn't land well."

It becomes:

"I'm slipping."
"I should be better than this."
"What's wrong with me?"

That shift from event to identity is where confidence erodes.

How Professionals Recover Cleanly

Confident professionals do not deny mistakes. They do something far more effective:
they contain them.

Containment looks like this:

- They name the error precisely without exaggeration
- They identify what was within their control
- They extract one learning
- They close the loop
- Then they stop

They do not:

- Ruminate
- Rehearse shame
- Carry the moment forward
- Downgrade their identity

The mistake is handled. The professional remains intact.

The "One-Line Recovery"

One of the most powerful recovery tools is also the simplest. After a mistake, professionals quietly say something like:

"That was a moment not a verdict." Or: "Information noted. Identity unchanged."

This isn't positive thinking. It's accurate thinking. The nervous system needs clarity, not comfort.

Why High Standards Make This Harder

Ironically, the people most affected by mistakes are often the best performers. They care.
They hold standards, they expect professionalism from themselves. The danger is when standards turn inward and become punishment. High standards should guide behaviour not attack identity.

Professionals keep standards external:

What will I do differently next time?

They do not internalise them as character judgement.

Letting the Day End

One of the quiet disciplines of confident professionals is this: They let days finish. Mistakes are reviewed once then the day is closed. They don't carry unfinished emotional business into tomorrow. They don't sleep with open loops running in their head. This doesn't happen by accident. It happens by choice.

A simple end-of-day question helps:

"What does not need to come with me into tomorrow?"

That question protects confidence more than any technique.

What This Changes Over Time

When mistakes are handled cleanly:

- Confidence stabilises
- Energy returns more quickly
- Judgement softens
- Performance becomes more consistent

Most importantly, the fear of making mistakes reduces. Not because mistakes stop happening
but because they stop being dangerous.

The Bigger Reframe

Here is the reframe that closes this chapter: Mistakes are not signs that you are losing confidence. They are signs that you are operating at the edge of complexity. People who never make mistakes are not confident. They are cautious. Professionals accept that occasional misjudgement is the price of engagement. Confidence is not perfection. It is recovery.

Bringing It Together

You do not need to stop making mistakes to stay confident. You need to stop attacking yourself for making them. When errors are treated as information rather than identity, confidence holds even when things go wrong. That is professional maturity.

Where We Go Next

Now that we've addressed mistakes and self-judgement, **Chapter 13** moves out a level. It looks at the patterns that shape confidence over months and years habits of thinking, reacting, and interpreting that either compound confidence or quietly undermine it. Because confidence isn't built in moments. It's built in patterns.

The Emotional Patterns That Shape Your Confidence

How Confidence Is Built or Undermined Over Time

This chapter steps back to look at the patterns that shape confidence over months and years. There's a particular kind of morning many salespeople recognise. Nothing has gone wrong yet, but something feels heavier than it should. You haven't met a customer, answered a call, or opened an email, and already the day feels like it will take more effort than usual.

Other mornings feel different. The work ahead may be demanding, but it feels manageable. You're not excited or energised just ready. The difference is rarely circumstances. It's the emotional pattern you're operating from.

The Layer Beneath Performance

Every salesperson carries emotional patterns habitual ways of interpreting, reacting to, and assigning meaning to what happens during the day. You don't consciously choose these patterns. You usually don't even notice them.

They run quietly in the background, shaping:

- How pressure lands
- How customers affect you
- How quickly confidence drains or recovers
- How heavy or light the work feels

Technique operates on the surface. Confidence lives underneath in these patterns. That's why two people can experience the same week the same customers, the same objections, the same outcomes and come away feeling very differently.

How Patterns Reveal Themselves Over Time

Emotional patterns rarely announce themselves in single moments. They show up across a run of days.

You notice them when:

- One difficult interaction seems to colour everything that follows
- A slow morning quietly drains your motivation for the entire day
- A small mistake lingers longer than it should
- Confidence feels harder to access by Thursday than it did on Monday

Nothing dramatic has happened but the accumulation is unmistakable. This is why confidence can feel solid one week and fragile the next, even when performance hasn't changed. The difference isn't ability. It's the pattern that's been quietly running underneath.

Where These Patterns Come From

These patterns weren't created in sales.

They were shaped earlier by:

- How stress was handled around you
- How mistakes were treated
- Whether reassurance felt conditional
- How authority and scrutiny showed up
- How uncertainty was tolerated

Sales doesn't invent these patterns. It activates them frequently and repeatedly. That's why selling can feel personal even when it isn't.

The Pattern of Anticipation

Some people start the day expecting friction. Others expect normality. This isn't optimism or pessimism. It's a pattern of anticipation.

When anticipation is threat-based, the mind scans constantly:

- Neutral expressions feel negative
- Hesitation feels like rejection
- Silence feels dangerous
- Quiet periods feel ominous

Over time, this creates fatigue not because the job is harder, but because vigilance never switches off. When anticipation is neutral or open, the same moments pass without charge. The nervous system isn't braced, so confidence has room to settle. Nothing external has changed. Only the lens.

The Pattern of Internal Pressure

Some salespeople carry pressure that doesn't come from targets, managers, or customers. It comes from inside.

A belief often unconscious that worth is measured by:

- Constant performance
- Constant responsiveness
- Constant output

This pattern makes normal fluctuations feel like warning signs. A quiet day becomes a referendum. A missed opportunity becomes evidence. Over weeks and months, this internal pressure quietly exhausts confidence even when results are good.

The Pattern of Emotional Absorption

Some people absorb the emotional state of whoever they're with. A confident customer lifts them, a hesitant one unsettles them, and a difficult one drains them. Across a day, this creates emotional whiplash. Across a season, it creates volatility and fatigue. Empathy is understanding another person's state. Absorption is taking it on. Professionals learn to read emotions without inheriting them. Their steadiness becomes the stabilising force in the interaction for both parties.

The Pattern of Self-Critique

Sales attracts people with standards, but standards often come with a harsh internal voice.

"You should know better."
"That wasn't good enough."
"You're slipping."

Over time, this voice doesn't sharpen performance it narrows confidence. Reflection becomes rumination. Learning turns into self-surveillance. The goal isn't to remove standards. It's to remove *self-attack* from the process.

The Pattern of Overinvestment

Some salespeople care so much that every interaction carries too much weight. They overthink, they overinterpret and they over attach to outcomes. This creates fragility over time. Confidence rises and falls with results instead of behaviour. Detachment doesn't mean caring less. It means allowing outcomes to be outcomes not verdicts on who you are.

The Deeper Pattern Beneath Them All

Every pattern ultimately traces back to one thing:

How you see yourself.

If your self-perception is steady capable, adaptable, professional then difficult periods are just periods. If it's fragile, those same periods feel like proof that something is wrong. Self-perception isn't fixed. It's shaped gradually by repetition, interpretation, and recovery.

How Patterns Actually Change

Patterns don't change through force or insight alone.

They change through:

- Noticing them without judgement
- Interrupting them gently
- Choosing differently in small moments
- Repeating that choice over time

This work isn't dramatic, but it's structural and structure is what confidence rests on.

Bringing It Together

Confidence isn't shaped by isolated moments. It's shaped by patterns the quiet, repeated ways you interpret, react, and recover over time. When those patterns soften and stabilise, confidence follows naturally. Not because you're trying to be confident but because there's less inside you undermining it.

Where We Go Next

Understanding patterns creates awareness. **Chapter 14** turns that awareness into rhythm the daily and weekly behaviours that quietly reinforce confidence until it becomes automatic. Not by effort. By consistency.

The Behaviours That Sustain Confidence

What Confident Professionals Do Consistently Even on Ordinary Days

This chapter translates awareness into daily and weekly behaviour. By now, confidence should no longer feel mysterious. You've seen how it's affected by pressure, rejection, fatigue, mistakes, and emotional patterns. You've seen how easily it erodes and how deliberately it can be protected.

What remains is this question:

What does confidence actually look like in daily behaviour?

Not in peak moments. Not when things are going well. But in the ordinary, repeatable actions that make confidence reliable rather than conditional. This chapter answers that question.

Confidence Is Visible Long Before It's Felt

One of the quiet truths about confidence is this: People often behave confidently before they feel confident. Behaviour leads state more often than the other way around. When professionals act with steadiness, clarity, and restraint, confidence follows naturally. That's why this chapter focuses on what confident professionals consistently do, rather than how they try to feel.

Presence: Being Fully Where You Are

Confident professionals are present. They are not distracted by the last conversation or preoccupied with the next one. Their attention is on the person in front of them, the words being said, and the moment unfolding.

Presence shows up as:

- Eye contact that's relaxed, not intense
- Listening without rehearsing replies
- Allowing moments to complete without rushing

Presence doesn't require effort. It requires attention, and attention is one of the strongest signals of confidence there is.

Pace: Slower Than Urgency, Faster Than Hesitation

Confident professionals control pace. They don't rush when pressure rises, and they don't stall when uncertainty appears. Their tempo remains steady even when the environment isn't.

This shows up in:

- Measured speech
- Deliberate movement
- Pauses that feel natural rather than forced

Pace regulation does more than calm others it stabilises your own thinking. When pace is controlled, confidence becomes easier to access.

Curiosity: Asking Before Explaining

Confident professionals are curious. They don't feel the need to immediately justify, correct, or persuade. They ask questions first not as a technique, but as a default stance.

Curiosity shows up as:

- Genuine interest in the customer's perspective
- Questions that clarify rather than challenge
- Openness to being wrong or incomplete

Curiosity reduces defensiveness on both sides of the conversation. It signals security rather than uncertainty.

Emotional Separation: Understanding Without Absorbing

Confident professionals understand others' emotions without inheriting them. They recognise anxiety, frustration, excitement, or hesitation but they don't let those emotions dictate their own state.

This separation allows them to:

- Stay calm with difficult customers
- Remain steady when others escalate
- Avoid emotional whiplash across the day

Empathy is the ability to recognise emotion; confidence is the discipline not to absorb it.

Firm Kindness: Calm Without Softness, Clear Without Aggression

One of the clearest markers of confidence is firm kindness.

Confident professionals are:

- Polite without being submissive
- Clear without being blunt
- Accommodating without over-giving

They don't confuse confidence with dominance or warmth with weakness. Firm kindness communicates: *"I respect you and I respect myself."* That balance is rare, and it's unmistakable.

Clean Language: Saying Less, Saying It Clearly

Confident professionals use clean language. They don't over-qualify, they don't hedge unnecessarily and they don't fill space with excess explanation.

Their language is:

- Simple
- Direct
- Proportionate to the moment

They trust that what they've said is enough and they allow silence to do its work. Clarity is a confidence amplifier.

Resetting: Returning to Centre Quickly

Confident professionals don't avoid wobble. They recover from it. When something doesn't land a question, a response, a moment they reset internally rather than spiralling.

This reset is usually quiet:

- A breath
- A pause
- A brief shift of posture
- A single grounding thought

Recovery speed matters more than perfection. Confidence is sustained not by never wobbling, but by returning to centre cleanly.

Consistency Over Intensity

What sustains confidence is not dramatic effort. It's consistency.

Confident professionals:

- Show up the same way on quiet days
- Maintain standards even when tired
- Regulate themselves without external prompts

Their confidence is predictable to others and to themselves and predictability is deeply reassuring.

How These Behaviours Work Together

None of these behaviours operates alone. Presence supports curiosity. Pace supports clarity. Emotional separation supports kindness. Reset supports consistency. Together, they form a behavioural posture a way of operating that makes confidence durable. This posture doesn't depend on: Mood or outcomes or energy, or even approval, it depends on practice.

Bringing It Together

Confidence is not something you summon. It's something you live into through behaviour.

When you consistently:

- Stay present
- Control pace
- Remain curious
- Separate emotion
- Communicate cleanly
- Reset quickly

Confidence stops being something you monitor. It becomes the background condition of how you work.

Where We Go Next

These behaviours don't just shape how you are they shape how you sound. In **Chapter 15**, we turn to communication: how confident professionals speak, frame conversations, and hold clarity without pressure. Because confidence isn't only visible in behaviour. It's audible in language.

Communicating With Confidence

How Confident Salespeople Sound, Speak, and Connect Without Forcing It

Confidence becomes visible through communication. How you speak, listen, pace, and hold silence is where internal confidence shows up externally. I once watched two salespeople handle almost identical customer conversations. Same product, same objection almost the same words. One closed the sale easily the other didn't. The difference wasn't what they said it was everything underneath the words.

The first salesperson spoke with a relaxed authority not loud, not dominant, just steady. When the customer raised a concern, she paused before responding. Her sentences had space in them. She asked questions and then genuinely waited for the answers, comfortable with the silence that followed. The customer leaned in, asked more questions, and bought.

The second salesperson said almost the same things, but his energy was different. He spoke quickly, filling every gap. His explanations were longer, more detailed, as if he was trying to convince himself as much as the customer. When the customer hesitated, he jumped in before they'd finished thinking. The customer pulled back, asked for time, and never returned.

Same words. Different outcomes. The variable wasn't product knowledge or sales technique. It was confidence and specifically how that confidence showed up in communication.

What Customers Actually Experience

Customers don't see your preparation. They don't see the inner work you've done, the self-talk you've improved, or the effort you put into staying composed. What they do experience instantly is how you communicate.

Your communication is the visible expression of your confidence. It shapes the emotional atmosphere of every interaction long before logic or facts come into play. Customers don't analyse tone, pace, or phrasing consciously. They feel something about you, and that feeling becomes the foundation for trust, safety, and decision-making.

This chapter isn't about sounding impressive. It's about sounding grounded. When your communication comes from steadiness rather than effort, everything becomes easier for you and for the customer.

Confidence Begins Before You Speak

Communication doesn't start when you open your mouth. It starts in the moment before you speak:

- The breath you take
- The posture you settle into
- The pace you choose
- The intention you hold

If your mind is rushing, your words will rush with it. If your mind is steady, your words naturally follow. Customers never see this internal adjustment, but they feel the outcome immediately. A calm salesperson is sensed before they're heard. That's why preparation isn't just about knowledge. It's about state. Your inner tone becomes your outer tone.

The Sound of Confidence

Confident communication has a recognisable quality. It's not loud, it's not dominant, it's not performative. It sounds like someone who has nothing to prove.

That sound has three characteristics:

1. **Calmness** because you're not trying to win the moment
2. **Clarity** because you've slowed your thinking enough to choose your words
3. **Completeness** because you allow a sentence to land

There's no scrambling. No apologetic tone. No over-explaining. Confidence sounds like someone who trusts their own thoughts and customers relax when they hear that.

Pace Is Emotional Regulation

Pace is one of the strongest signals of confidence in communication. Rushed speech communicates pressure, even when the words are right. It signals anxiety, fear of losing the customer, or fear of silence. A steady pace communicates the opposite:

"I'm comfortable here. We have time. We can do this properly."

A confident salesperson isn't slow they're *measured*. And here's the part most people miss:
customers mirror pace. When you rush, they tense. When you slow, they settle. That isn't persuasion. That's emotional regulation.

Simplicity as Mastery

Confident communicators don't use complexity to sound knowledgeable. They use simplicity.

"This is how it works."

"This is the part that matters."

"This is my recommendation."

Simplicity communicates mastery because it shows you understand something well enough to make it easy for someone else. Complexity often hides uncertainty. Clarity reveals confidence. Confident communicators remove clutter. Insecure communicators add it.

Listening as Strength

Confident people listen differently. They're not waiting for their turn. They're not rehearsing their next line. They're not threatened by what the customer might say. They listen fully to words, tone, hesitation, and emotion.

That kind of listening communicates something powerful: "I'm here. I can handle this. You don't need to defend yourself." Listening isn't passive. Listening is emotional strength. Customers trust people who listen with composure, because composure signals safety.

Questions and Silence

Confident salespeople don't ask questions nervously or apologetically. They ask purposeful questions gently, but with intent:

"What's most important to you here?"
"What would make this feel like the right decision?"
"What needs to happen for this to work?"

These questions communicate authority and respect. And then confident communicators do something many people find uncomfortable. They stop talking, they allow silence, they let the customer think and they don't rush to rescue the moment. Silence isn't empty. Silence is where decisions form. Being able to hold silence without anxiety is one of the clearest signals of confidence there is.

Honest Communication Builds Trust

Confident communication doesn't avoid truth. It includes it.

"Here's the limitation you should know about."
"This won't suit everyone."
"Let me give you the straightforward answer."

Honesty isn't risky when it comes from steadiness. Customers hear transparency as competence. They trust people who aren't afraid of the truth because those people don't sound desperate for the outcome. Confidence doesn't hide reality. It's comfortable with it.

Closing With Calm Clarity

Closing isn't about pressure. It's about clarity.

"Here's what I recommend next."
"Would you like to go ahead?"
"Shall we organise that now?"

No drama. No artificial urgency. No performance. A confident close respects the customer and respects your role. When the conversation has been steady throughout, the close feels like a natural conclusion, not a push.

What Customers Feel Not What You Say

When you communicate with confidence, customers feel:

- Understood
- Guided
- Safe
- Informed
- Unpressured

Your communication becomes the emotional container they make decisions inside. That's why confident communication isn't a soft skill. It's a commercial one. Confidence is communication. Communication is confidence. They're the same thing, expressed differently.

Where We Go Next

Confident communication builds trust in the moment. In **Chapter 16**, we take the final step how trust, consistency, and professionalism turn confidence into long-term customer relationships. Confidence opens the door. Trust is why customers come back.

Trust, Consistency, and Long-Term Relationships

How Confident Salespeople Turn One Conversation Into a Lifetime of Business

This chapter moves beyond individual conversations to the arc of a sales career. Confidence might open the door in sales. Trust is what keeps it open. Confidence helps you handle the first conversation well. Trust determines whether the customer comes back, refers others, and chooses you again years later. Confidence influences moments. Trust shapes careers.

This chapter is about how that trust is built not through tactics or charm, but through steady, predictable behaviour repeated over time. Because confidence makes you effective. Trust makes you valuable.

How Trust Actually Forms

Trust doesn't arrive in a single interaction. It forms quietly, across dozens of ordinary moments. I've worked with a financial advisor for more than fifteen years. I can't pinpoint when he stopped being a financial advisor and became my financial advisor the shift happened gradually, through consistency rather than brilliance.

The first meeting was fine. Professional. Clear. No pressure. Nothing remarkable. But then something small happened. He called back exactly when he said he would with the information he'd promised. No delay. No excuse. No drama. Later, when I asked about a more complex investment option, he surprised me. "Based on what you've told me," He said, "I don't think that's right for you. There's a simpler option that probably suits you better."

It was the less expensive choice. The smaller commission. The honest answer. That was the moment trust began to deepen. Not trust that he'd always be right, nobody is but trust that he would tell me the truth as he saw it, even when it wasn't in his immediate interest. That is what trust feels like from the customer's side.

Trust Is Emotional, Not Logical

Customers don't trust you because your argument is perfect.

They trust you because they feel:

- Safe
- Understood
- Respected
- Guided rather than pushed
- Free to think

Trust emerges when customers experience you as:

- Consistent in tone
- Steady under pressure
- Honest even when it's inconvenient
- Transparent about risks
- Reliable across interactions

Trust isn't a moment, it's a pattern and patterns are built through repetition, not performance.

Being Liked vs Being Trusted

Many salespeople confuse being liked with being trusted. Being liked is about warmth, being trusted is about credibility. Being liked feels good, being trusted builds careers.

Salespeople who chase likeability often:

- Soften difficult truths
- Avoid challenge
- Downplay downsides
- Over-reassure
- Hesitate to recommend against a sale

Customers may enjoy the interaction but something essential is missing. At a subtle level, they sense that the salesperson is managing the mood rather than helping them decide.

Trusted professionals are willing to be:

- Clear
- Direct
- Honest
- Occasionally uncomfortable

Customers may not like every moment, but they respect it. And respect is what trust grows from.

Consistency: The Backbone of Trust

Trust accelerates when customers experience the same professionalism from you every time.

- Same pace
- Same tone
- Same clarity
- Same courtesy
- Same honesty

Inconsistent behaviour creates anxiety. When customers don't know which version of you, they'll get calm or rushed, attentive or distracted they stay guarded. They keep evaluating. But when you are consistent, customers relax. You become predictable in the best possible way. Consistency doesn't impress. It reassures and reassurance is what allows relationships to deepen.

Honesty as a Confidence Multiplier

Honesty real honesty is one of the strongest trust-builders available to any salesperson.

"This option isn't right for everyone."
"You probably don't need the premium version."
"If you're unsure, I'd recommend thinking it through."
"Here's the downside you should know about."

Most customers are conditioned to expect spin. When they encounter calm, grounded honesty, it stands out immediately. Honesty delivered without drama doesn't weaken your position. It strengthens it. Customers stop guarding themselves. They stop searching for hidden motives. They start engaging openly. Honesty is confidence expressed externally.

Reliability: Trust in Motion

Trust isn't built through big gestures.

It's built through small commitments kept:

- Calling when you said you would
- Sending what you promised
- Remembering details
- Being punctual
- Closing loops cleanly

Individually, these actions seem unremarkable. Collectively, they create something powerful.

Most people live in a world where follow-through is casual. When you become reliably dependable, you become trusted. Reliability isn't glamorous. But it creates repeat business, referrals, and long-term loyalty that no technique can replace.

Guiding, Not Controlling

Customers don't want to be controlled. They want to be guided.

Guidance sounds like:

"Here's the next logical step."

"Based on what you've said, this seems the right direction."

"Let's take this one stage at a time."

Control feels urgent and forceful. Guidance feels calm and respectful. When customers feel guided, they stop defending. They let you lead. And in that moment, you stop being a salesperson and become an advisor. Advisors get chosen again.

Stability: The Quiet Trust Builder

Customers may arrive anxious, uncertain, or under pressure. You remain steady, you don't absorb their emotion, you don't mirror their stress, and you don't rush to fix their mood. That steadiness becomes the emotional anchor in the interaction. Stability tells the customer:

"You're safe here. You can think. I'm not adding pressure."

Few things build trust faster than being calm when others aren't.

Becoming "Their Person"

When trust is built consistently, something shifts. You stop being a salesperson, you become their salesperson. The first call, the trusted voice, the referral. This doesn't happen through brilliance or persuasion. It happens through professionalism repeated so often it becomes reputation. Trust turns confidence into relationship. Relationship turns skill into reputation. Reputation creates a career that sustains itself.

Bringing It Together

The strongest sales careers are built quietly. Not on charisma. Not on pressure. Not on clever techniques.

They're built on:

- Consistency
- Honesty
- Reliability
- Calm guidance
- Emotional steadiness

Confidence opens doors. Trust keeps them open.

Where We Go Next

Trust is built over time and protecting the confidence required to sustain that trust is a mindset challenge. In **Chapter 17**, we move into how confident professionals think, adapt, and stay grounded across entire careers not just good weeks or strong seasons. Because long-term trust requires long-term steadiness.

CHAPTER 17:

Thinking Like a Confident Professional

How to Build a Mindset That Supports You for a Lifetime in Sales

This chapter focuses on the mindset that allows confidence to endure across decades, not just seasons. A confident day is helpful. A confident week is encouraging. But a confident career is something else entirely. Sales is one of the few professions where your thinking is tested daily sometimes hourly. Outcomes are visible. Rejection is frequent. Pressure is constant. If the way you interpret events isn't stable, confidence slowly erodes, even when skill remains high. This chapter isn't about positive thinking or motivation. It's about the mental posture that allows confidence to endure.

The Invisible Difference That Separates Careers

Two salespeople can have:

- The same training
- The same product knowledge
- The same customer base

One stays confident for decades. The other burns out, plateaus, or becomes brittle. The difference isn't talent. It's how they interpret what happens. Not consciously but habitually. Confident professionals don't experience fewer challenges. They experience the same events through a different lens.

Emotional Thinking vs Professional Thinking

Most people begin sales using an emotional mindset.

In this mindset:

- Good days confirm worth
- Bad days threaten identity
- Rejection feels personal
- Quiet periods feel ominous
- Difficult customers feel like judgement

It's understandable. Sales is human work. But emotional thinking is unstable over time. It turns confidence into something reactive something that rises and falls with circumstances.

Professional thinking works differently.

In a professional mindset:

- Good days reflect momentum, not who you are
- Bad days show challenge, not deficiency
- Rejection is part of the landscape
- Quiet periods are expected within cycles
- Difficult customers reflect their own state

The same events occur, but confidence remains intact.

How Professionals Interpret What Happens

When a sale is lost, the professional doesn't ask:

"What's wrong with me?"

They ask:

"What didn't align?"

Timing. Budget. Need. Fit. External factors. They use this to learn and correct. The outcome becomes information not a verdict. When a day is slow, they don't write stories about decline. They recognise sales cycles. Sales has seasons, cycles, quiet Tuesdays, slow Octobers, unpredictable weeks. Professionals expect this. Their confidence isn't surprised by normal variation. When a customer is difficult, they don't absorb it. They maintain separation.

"This is their state, not my worth."

That single distinction prevents emotional contagion and allows the professional to stay steady while the customer settles.

Mistakes Without Self-Attack

One of the clearest signs of professional thinking is how mistakes are handled. Professionals don't deny mistakes. They don't dramatise them either.

A mistake becomes:

- Specific
- Contained
- Instructive

"What exactly went wrong?"
"What will I adjust?"
"Move on."

There's no character assassination. No identity erosion. Confidence survives because it was never placed on the line.

Results Without Inflation or Collapse

Interestingly, professionals also interpret success differently. Strong results don't inflate identity. Average results don't deflate it.

Professionals understand that outcomes fluctuate based on:

- Timing
- Market conditions
- Customer readiness
- Factors outside their control

They focus on standards, not spikes. This is why their confidence doesn't collapse when numbers dip and doesn't become fragile when numbers soar.

Pressure Without Catastrophe

Pressure reveals thinking patterns quickly. Under pressure, emotional thinking says:

"Everything depends on this."
"I can't mess this up."

Professional thinking narrows focus:

"Pressure is present."
"My job is to stay steady and execute my process."

Professionals don't deny stakes; they refuse to amplify them and that restraint alone protects confidence.

Comparison Without Damage

Professionals notice others' success without using it as a weapon against themselves.

They understand:

- Different territories
- Different experience levels
- Different strengths
- Different circumstances

The only meaningful comparison is internal:

Am I improving? Am I learning? Am I steadier than I was?

That orientation keeps confidence developmental, not competitive.

Uncertainty Without Anxiety

The future is uncertain in every sales career. Markets change. Industries evolve. Conditions shift.

Professionals accept uncertainty as permanent and focus on what they control:

- Skill
- Behaviour
- Relationships
- Adaptability

Worry doesn't prepare you. Competence does. This thinking removes anxiety without removing responsibility.

The Core Separation That Changes Everything

Across all these situations, professional thinking does one thing consistently:

It separates:

- The job from identity
- The moment from worth
- The customer's state from the professional's state
- Short-term outcomes from long-term trajectory

That separation creates emotional space, and emotional space is where sustainable confidence lives.

How This Way of Thinking Develops

Professional thinking isn't adopted overnight.

It's built through:

- Noticing emotional interpretations
- Pausing before believing them
- Choosing a more useful frame
- Returning to action
- Repeating thousands of times

Gradually, the emotional reaction loses authority. The professional interpretation becomes default not because you've eliminated emotion but because you've learned not to treat it as truth.

The Mindset That Lasts

Professionals who sustain confidence over decades see sales as:

- A craft, not a performance
- A relationship, not a transaction
- A practice, not a judgement

They guide rather than convince, they interpret rather than react and they stay steady rather than brittle. Sales remains demanding, but confidence becomes stable.

Bringing It Together

Confidence that lasts isn't about being upbeat or always thinking positively. It's about thinking clearly under pressure. When you stop turning events into identity, stop turning outcomes into verdicts, and stop treating emotion as evidence, confidence becomes something you think with, not something you chase.

Where We Go Next

In **Chapter 18**, we bring everything together. You'll see how confidence operates as a cycle something you can return to, reinforce, and renew whenever pressure, fatigue, or change begins to wear it down. Not as motivation. As structure.

The Confidence Cycle

How to Protect, Renew, and Strengthen Your Confidence for Life

Everything in this book fits inside this cycle. Once you understand it, confidence stops feeling fragile. Confidence doesn't stand still, it moves, it rises and falls. It strengthens, dips, and returns. That's why confident professionals don't chase a permanent state they understand a cycle they can return to whenever pressure, doubt, or fatigue appears. This book has never been about eliminating difficult moments. It has been about knowing what to do when they arrive. That understanding changes everything.

Coming Full Circle

Remember the young woman from the beginning of the book. Standing in the doorway.
Three seconds of hesitation. That brief moment where uncertainty threatened to decide her behaviour. That moment hasn't disappeared. It still shows up for her, and for everyone who does this work. What changed wasn't the absence of uncertainty. It was her relationship to it.

She learned that confidence isn't something you wait to feel. It's something you create, moment by moment, through a reliable process. That process is the confidence cycle.

Confidence as a Cycle Not a Trait

Confident people are not confident all the time, they experience pressure, they feel doubt, they lose deals and they have difficult days. What separates them is not emotional immunity it's structure.

They know how confidence is:

- Prepared
- Expressed
- Tested
- Restored
- Renewed

So, when confidence dips, they don't panic, they recognise where they are in the cycle and return to it.

The Four Movements of the Cycle

1. Preparation: Confidence begins with preparation. Not rituals, not motivation, but a deliberate choice about how you show up. A few quiet minutes, a settled pace, an intention to be steady rather than reactive. Preparation sets the tone before the day gets a chance to set it for you.

2. Presence: Confidence then moves into presence. The customer arrives; the conversation begins. You stay with what's happening rather than what you fear might happen, you listen, you slow your pace and you don't absorb the other person's state. Confidence becomes visible through behaviour. Then come the tests. A lost sale, a difficult customer, a mistake or a moment where something doesn't land. This is where confidence is often lost unless you understand the cycle.

3. Recovery: The next part of the cycle is recovery. You contain the moment; you extract what's useful, you release the rest and you reset. One interaction doesn't contaminate the next.

4. Renewal: Finally comes renewal, at the end of the day, at the end of the week, at the end of a season. You don't carry everything forward; you keep the learning and let the emotional weight go. This is how confidence stays light enough to sustain. Then the cycle begins again.

Why This Changes Everything

Once you understand the cycle:

- Confidence no longer feels fragile
- Dips stop feeling dangerous
- Bad days stop feeling terminal
- Pressure loses its edge

You stop expecting to arrive at confidence and start trusting your ability to return to it.

That trust is the real foundation of professional confidence.

The Quiet Transformation

Six months after that first moment in the doorway, I watched the same woman greet customers with calm, grounded presence. Not because she'd eliminated uncertainty. But because she knew what to do with it.

- A breath
- A pause
- A choice of pace
- Then forward

Later, I saw her training someone new. "The first few weeks are uncomfortable," she said.

"That's normal. Your system is learning this is safe. If you prepare, stay present, reset after difficult moments, and let the day end it gets steadily easier." She wasn't repeating theory. She was describing the cycle now part of who she was.

What You Carry Forward

You don't need to remember everything in this book. You don't need to do everything perfectly. You just need to remember this: Confidence is not a feeling you hope appears.

It's a system you know how to return to.

- Preparation
- Presence
- Recovery
- Renewal

When confidence dips you don't judge it. You re-enter the cycle, that's how confidence lasts.

A Final Word

The strongest professionals aren't confident because they never wobble. They're confident because they know how to come back, calmly, cleanly, without drama. You know how to do that now, and that knowledge doesn't fade with time. It deepens with use.

Confidence isn't something you find. It's something you build, protect, and renew, again and again, through the cycle.

A Final Invitation

If this book has resonated with you, it's likely because you recognise that confidence in sales is not about personality, motivation, or performance. It's about how you manage yourself under real conditions.

Everything in this book is designed to help you build that steadiness deliberately not for a single conversation, but for a career.

If you'd like to explore this work further, Breakthrough Change Management works with sales professionals, leadership teams, and organisations to develop calm, credible confidence under pressure. This includes individual coaching, team development, and practical behavioural programmes built for real-world sales environments.

You can find further resources, articles, and information at:

www.breakthroughchangemanagement.com

For professional enquiries, training, or coaching programmes:

info@breakthroughchangemanagement.com

This book is not the end of the work. It's the foundation. What you do with it next is where confidence becomes permanent.

About the Author

J. M. Walsh is a leadership and behavioural development specialist with extensive experience working with sales professionals, leadership teams, and complex organisations. His work focuses on confidence under pressure, professional presence, and the behavioural foundations of high performance.

Through Breakthrough Change Management, he supports individuals and teams in building clarity, composure, and reliability in demanding environments.

Further Reading

This book is grounded in practical experience rather than theory. However, many of the ideas explored here align with well-established research in psychology, behaviour, and professional performance. The following titles provide useful additional context for readers who wish to explore these themes further.

The following books offer useful perspectives on psychology, behaviour, confidence, and performance under pressure. They are not required reading, but they support many of the themes explored in this book.

Psychology, Behaviour, and the Mind

- **Thinking, Fast and Slow** – Daniel Kahneman
  Insight into how humans make decisions under uncertainty and pressure.
- **The Chimp Paradox** – Prof. Steve Peters
  A practical explanation of emotional responses and self-regulation.
- **Emotional Intelligence** – Daniel Goleman
  Foundational work on emotional awareness and regulation in professional life.
- **Why Zebras Don't Get Ulcers** – Robert Sapolsky
  A clear explanation of stress, biology, and the nervous system.

Confidence, Performance, and Pressure

- **Mindset** – Carol Dweck
  Understanding growth, learning, and identity without fragility.
- **Peak** – Anders Ericsson
  How deliberate practice builds reliable performance over time.

- **The Inner Game of Tennis** – W. Timothy Gallwey
  A classic on quiet confidence, attention, and self-interference.

Professional Presence, Leadership, and Influence

- **Leadership and Self-Deception** – The Arbinger Institute
  Insight into how internal states shape behaviour and perception.
- **Quiet** – Susan Cain
  Reframing confidence beyond loud or performative models.
- **The Trusted Advisor** – David Maister, Charles Green & Robert Galford
  Trust, credibility, and professionalism in advisory relationships.

Sales (Aligned, Not Tactical)

- **Let's Get Real or Let's Not Play** – Mahan Khalsa
  Integrity-based selling and professional clarity.
- **The Challenger Sale** – Matthew Dixon & Brent Adamson
  Insight into sales behaviour under pressure (read critically, not dogmatically).

Sales Confidence That Lasts

How Professionals Stay Calm, Credible, and in Control Under Pressure

Sales is uncomfortable even when you're good at it.
If you've ever felt pressure, self-doubt, or emotional fatigue in sales, this book will feel uncomfortably familiar.

The truth is sales tests more than skill.
It tests composure, identity, and emotional resilience day after day.

Sales Confidence That Lasts is not about motivation, scripts, or "positive thinking". It's a practical guide to building confidence that holds steady under real-world conditions: rejection, uncertainty, quiet periods, difficult customers, and high expectations.

This book shows you how confident professionals actually operate not by eliminating discomfort, but by learning how to manage themselves inside it.

In this book, you'll learn how to:

- Stay calm and credible when you're being judged
- Handle rejection without carrying it into the next conversation
- Manage quiet days without losing momentum or confidence
- Deal with difficult customers without absorbing their emotions
- Recover from mistakes without self-criticism or doubt
- Build confidence as a professional identity, not a fragile feeling

There are no gimmicks here. No scripts. No performance tricks.
Just clear thinking, practical frameworks, and a grounded approach to confidence that works over the long term.

If you sell in the real world and you want confidence you can rely on, not perform **this book is for you.**

www.ingramcontent.com/pod-product-compliance
Lightning Source LLC
Chambersburg PA
CBHW071603200326
41519CB00021BB/6855